"While following the author's creative focus through so many theological and ecological sources in this work; I was reminded of Soren Kierkegaard's remark that the sign of a true artist is not so much the creative flights of genius but how solidly, how tenderly, he returns to touch the earth. In Owen Cummings' book, we are brought prayerfully and tenderly to the One '*in the within of all things in the universe.*'"

—**Peter McCarthy**, OCSO, abbot,
Our Lady of Guadalupe Trappist Abbey

"Living in a county that touts itself as 'The Eden at the End of the Oregon Trail' and with access to a well-stocked library, Owen Cummings has written an encompassing and concentrated book on the history of the theology of creation from the perspective of praise and gratitude. He writes lucidly for educated readers, urging them to understand creation as God's ongoing gift and to respond to that gift in grateful prayer."

—**Hugh Feiss**, OSB, co-editor of *A Benedictine Reader*

"Owen Cummings, steeped in theological tradition, has written this book for those who are not. The scholar will of course recognize the broad contours of their discipline; Christians everywhere will recognize the broad contours of their own faith-experience. The author masterfully guides the reader into a panoramic vision of all that Creation should mean. Throughout it all, this work remains true to the stated purpose, as it 'leads others to praise this God from whom all blessing flows.'"

—**Andrew C. Cummings**, professor of philosophy,
Mount Angel Seminary

"My friend Deacon Owen Cummings, through his newest work, *How Great Thou Art!*, has once again sparked a renewed sense of gratitude in me for the wonder of all of God's creation, with a special emphasis on our common home, Mother Earth. I am certain that those who read *How Great Thou Art!* will inevitably grow in a heartfelt response of thanksgiving to our God whose creative energy knows no bounds."

—**John C. Wester**, archbishop of Santa Fe

"*How Great Thou Art!* is a work of profound scholarship. It traces in an impressive manner the topic of creation through the Old and New Testaments, the patristic and medieval periods, to the present. The book is not simply a history of the topic of creation, but a masterful and learned interpretation of an increasingly pressing subject. I could not recommend this book highly enough. It is Owen Cummings at his best."

—**M. Francis Mannion**, pastor emeritus, St. Vincent de Paul Parish

How Great Thou Art!

How Great Thou Art!

Theological Perspectives on Creation

OWEN F. CUMMINGS

CASCADE *Books* • Eugene, Oregon

HOW GREAT THOU ART!
Theological Perspectives on Creation

Copyright © 2024 Owen F. Cummings. All rights reserved. Except for brief quotations in critical publications or reviews, no part of this book may be reproduced in any manner without prior written permission from the publisher. Write: Permissions, Wipf and Stock Publishers, 199 W. 8th Ave., Suite 3, Eugene, OR 97401.

Cascade Books
An Imprint of Wipf and Stock Publishers
199 W. 8th Ave., Suite 3
Eugene, OR 97401

www.wipfandstock.com

PAPERBACK ISBN: 979-8-3852-1531-7
HARDCOVER ISBN: 979-8-3852-1532-4
EBOOK ISBN: 979-8-3852-1533-1

Cataloguing-in-Publication data:

Names: Cummings, Owen F. [author].

Title: How great thou art! : theological perspectives on creation / by Owen F. Cummings.

Description: Eugene, OR: Cascade Books, 2024 | Includes bibliographical references.

Identifiers: ISBN 979-8-3852-1531-7 (paperback) | ISBN 979-8-3852-1532-4 (hardcover) | ISBN 979-8-3852-1533-1 (ebook)

Subjects: LCSH: Creation. | Creation—History of doctrines. | Theology, Doctrinal.

Classification: BT695 C866 2024 (paperback) | BT695 (ebook)

VERSION NUMBER 08/07/24

Dedicated to:

Cathy
Andrew
Anne
Owen
Susan
Mary

Contents

1 How Great Thou Art! | 1
2 Creation in the Old Testament | 5
3 Creation in the New Testament | 23
4 Creation in the Christian Tradition: The Patristic and Medieval Periods | 30
5 Creation in the Christian Tradition: From the Renaissance to Pope Francis's *Laudato Si* | 54
6 A Sprinkling of Contemporary Theologians on Creation | 68
7 The Mystery of Evil and Suffering | 96
8 Conclusion | 111

Bibliography | 115

1

How Great Thou Art!

> What does it mean to say that the universe is "created"? Is there a purpose or meaning to our existence? What explains the fact that there is something rather than nothing? Or is existence just a brute fact? Such persistent and fundamental questions prompted the human imagination to look for clues within the universe for a more essential source of existence that is not part of the universe.
>
> Simon Oliver[1]

> How can we imagine the gracious, compassionate love of God for the created world?
>
> Elizabeth A. Johnson[2]

> Christian reflection on creation has been a bit of a Cinderella in twentieth-century theology—at least until the last few years, when a variety of pressures has brought it very much to the fore.
>
> Rowan D. Williams[3]

THE QUESTIONS RAISED BY theologian Simon Oliver probably occur to many people at least at some time in their lives. They may

---

1. Oliver, *Creation*, 1.
2. Johnson, *Creation and the Cross*, xi.
3. Williams, "On Being Creatures," 63.

not be expressed in quite the same way as Oliver. Indeed, they may be but momentary ripples on the surface of some days, days good and marked by life-giving joy, days not so good and characterized by trouble, sadness, trauma, or perhaps just tedium. These are some of the issues that impinge upon the theology of creation. In our time, however, these existential questions about creation have an added edge to them in the light of radical climate change, something alluded to (among other things) by Rowan Williams above. As I write during the summer of 2023 and into 2024, climatologists tell us that 2023 is the hottest year on record. Planet earth is in peril. This realization has issued in greater awareness of the theology of creation, leading, for example, to Pope Francis's encyclical letter *Laudato Si* (2015), which has received positive endorsement across the ecumenical spectrum.[4] Along the lines of Pope Francis's thinking, opening his recent book *Creation*, theologian David Fergusson writes: "Above all, awareness of the fragility of the Earth's ecosystem and the damage that is caused it by human populations has led to a much greater concentration on the theme of creation in contemporary theology.... An overriding conviction is that the doctrine of creation has suffered from inadequate exposure in the history of the church because it has too long been merely the stage for the enactment of the theology of sin and redemption."[5]

There have been many fine publications on the theology of creation. So, it might be asked, "Why another one?" Among various personal answers to this question I have as a major response the desire to make more accessible to the Christian reading public some of the enormous riches of the Christian tradition on the theology of creation. While I write as a Catholic theologian, I hope that my approach to creation may be helpful to Christians from other traditions. Hardly necessary to point out, no one person can address all the aspects of creation—the Scriptures, all the relevant

---

4. Among the many commentaries on theology and ecology and especially with regard to Pope Francis's encyclical letter, I would highlight two superb publications of Kevin Irwin: *A Commentary on Laudato Si* and *Ecology, Liturgy and the Sacraments*.

5. Fergusson, *Creation*, 1.

Christian authors over two millennia, all the exciting contemporary scientific insights, the many moral issues both personal and social-political. Selectivity is necessary and in what follows in this little book readers will see my selectivity at work and will thereby come to recognize my theological direction and bias. My hope, however, is that this minor contribution will prove helpful.

As already noted, there are many fine books on the theology of creation, many of which are easily enough available through the normal channels. I think it would be fair to say that many approaches to the theology of creation are problem-centered. The problems are varied, for example, the new cosmologies and creation, the integration of evolution and ecological concerns into theology, more recent work on Scripture and historical theology, the challenges of evil and suffering, and so forth. All such approaches are meaningful, and indeed, necessary. If we are to say what we believe to be true, to be the case, there will be a necessary, defensive element to our speaking.

This book is a little different. Its perspective is primarily one of prayer, praise, and gratitude, all of which are seen as integrally related—I am thinking of Elizabeth Johnson's rhetorical question opening this introductory chapter, "How can we imagine the gracious, compassionate love of God for the created world?" Of course, this book is informed by recent (as well as not so recent!) approaches to a Christian understanding of creation, but the intention throughout is to highlight prayer, praise, and gratitude to God, to move in the direction of seeing creation as both gift and "sacrament," and to invite us toward mystical transformation. This does not make it a devotional book simply, although that would indeed please the author, but rather it is a reading of the Christian tradition oriented to praising and thanking the Creator.

That reading is captured in the first stanza of the well-known hymn "How Great Thou Art," composed by Carl Boberg in 1885:

> *O Lord, my God, when I in awesome wonder*
> *Consider all the worlds Thy hands have made,*
> *I see the stars, I hear the rolling thunder,*
> *Thy power throughout the universe displayed.*

How Great Thou Art

*Then sings my soul, my Savior God to Thee
How great Thou art, how great Thou art.*

I agree with theologians Daniel W. Hardy and David F. Ford that "praising God, recognizing him as God in feeling, word and action, is a key to the ecology in which right knowledge of God grows."[6] Over fifty years and more of studying and teaching theology I have come to dislike those theological approaches that separate out too much systematic theology and Scripture, and systematic theology and spirituality. In this little book I hope to overcome in some degree those separations, and so I would be so pleased if this little book leads others to praise this God from whom all blessing flows.

---

6. Hardy and Ford, *Jubilate*, 112. The theme of praise runs throughout this beautiful book.

2

Creation in the Old Testament

> *Both creation stories in the early chapters of Genesis are narratives of grace. The making of the world in Genesis 1 is a free and unconstrained act of God. There is no sense of divine compulsion or necessity, nor is there any description of struggle.*
>
> David Fergusson[1]

IT SEEMS TO BE the case that Israel experienced God at work in saving and guiding his people and then only later came to an understanding of God as Creator. Thus, what appears to be an early kind of "creed" is found with this emphasis in Deuteronomy 26:5–9:

> A wandering Aramaean was my ancestor; he went down into Egypt and lived there as an alien, few in number, and there he became a great nation, mighty and populous. When the Egyptians treated us harshly and afflicted us, by imposing hard labor on us, we cried to the LORD, the God of our ancestors; the LORD heard our voice and saw our affliction, our toil, and our oppression. The LORD brought us out of Egypt with a mighty hand and an outstretched arm, with a terrifying display of power, and with signs and

---

1. Fergusson, *Creation*, 4.

wonders; and he brought us into this place and gave us this land, a land flowing with milk and honey.

In other words, God's saving hand with his people, their experience of what we might call salvation history, comes chronologically before they reached an understanding of God as Creator. Robert Butterworth writes: "It was because God could exercise such obvious mastery over the events and course of history as he displayed in his saving actions for Israel that in time Israel came to see that he exercised a similar—but wider—mastery over the whole of nature."[2] When the Hebrews did reach toward the theology of creation, that theology found outstanding expression in the poetic creation narratives of Genesis 1–2.

The Genesis Creation Narratives: Introduction

It would be difficult to contradict the description of the Genesis creation narratives offered by Joseph Ratzinger when he says: "These words, with which Holy Scripture begins, always have the effect on me of the solemn tolling of a great old bell, which stirs the heart from afar with its beauty and dignity and gives it an inkling of the mystery of eternity."[3] The sound of the texts especially when read aloud, slowly and carefully, draw us almost inexorably to the mystery of God. They begin the magnificent symphony of Scripture that is the Liturgy of the Word at the Easter Vigil. The words of the creation narrative have made their way deep into the Catholic imagination and even when people may have walked away from the church they often still remember these words of creation spoken in the book of Genesis.

The multiple source or documentary theory of the Pentateuch goes back to the nineteenth-century biblical critics. Today Old Testament scholars present different reactions to the documentary hypothesis, but our concern in this book on the theology

---

2. Butterworth, *Theology of Creation*, 26.
3. Ratzinger, *"In the Beginning . . . ,"* 3.

of creation presumes something like it.[4] Very briefly, the documentary hypothesis affirms four traditions—whether those traditions are judged to be oral or written or both is of no concern to us here—behind the Pentateuch:

J = the Yahwist tradition

E = the Elohist tradition

D = the Deuteronomist tradition

P = the Priestly tradition

There are two creation narratives in the book of Genesis: Genesis 1:1—2:4a, taken as representing the Priestly tradition (P), and Genesis 2:4b–25, representing the Yahwist tradition (J). Since the Priestly account of creation comes in the text before the Yahwist in Genesis, we shall turn to it first.

The Priestly Narrative of Creation: Genesis 1:1—2:4a

This text is the very first reading in the Liturgy of the Word for the Easter Vigil celebration. That is as it should be. We begin this holiest of Christian celebrations with the moment when God speaks all of creation into being. We are reaching back billions of years to the very first moment.

The final reading, the Gospel reading, is from the earliest gospel, that of St. Mark 16:1–7:

> When the sabbath was over, Mary Magdalene, Mary, the mother of James, and Salome bought spices so that they might go and anoint him.
>
> Very early when the sun had risen, on the first day of the week, they came to the tomb. They were saying to one another, "Who will roll back the stone for us from the entrance to the tomb?" When they looked up, they saw that the stone had been rolled back; it was very large.

---

4. A very fair and balanced perspective on the documentary hypothesis may be found in Collins, *Introduction to the Hebrew Bible*, 49–68.

> On entering the tomb they saw a young man sitting on the right side, clothed in a white robe, and they were utterly amazed. He said to them, "Do not be amazed! You seek Jesus of Nazareth, the crucified. He has been raised; he is not here."

"He is not here." Resurrection has occurred. The Risen Jesus we may say has reached—through the resurrection—the point to which all creation aspires, final communion in and with God. So the Liturgy of the Word at the Easter Vigil begins with creation and ends with consummation. Creation and Christology come together, belong together.

It is important at this point to open your Bible and to read through this narrative for yourself. Having refreshed your memory, the comments that follow now will make more sense. The Priestly author or editor remains anonymous, nowhere named in the text. The author/editor/source is probably to be dated at the time of the exile in Babylon (ca. 587–538 BCE). Arguably this is the period when many of the texts that have come down to us as the Old Testament were put, at least initially, into written form. The catastrophe of the exile called forth from the people and especially from their theological leaders new and deeper responses to their already existing faith in God as Savior.

Throughout this creation narrative of "P," the Creator is called *Elohim* (God), in distinction to the name *Yahweh*. God creates through speech, thus providing an emphasis on God's transcendent character, or an emphasis on the power of God's word, such as we find in Deutero-Isaiah (Isa 55:10–12). Not only is God's transcendence emphasized by his speaking creation into being, but also by his ontological superiority, if we may put it like that, over the heavenly bodies that were thought to be divine in some fashion throughout the ancient Near East, and to control human affairs. God is creator of these heavenly bodies too. Theologian Leo Scheffczyk writes:

> The anti-mythical character of the Priestly Creation narrative is especially clear where the creation of the heavenly bodies is related (Genesis 1:14–19); for mythological

thought always tended to look on these bodies as godlike beings, independent of the creator's power, whereas the Priestly Code represents both light and the heavenly bodies as lacking any creative power of their own. . . . The anti-mythical character of the Priestly Code is even more pronounced in the narrative of the fourth day of creation, which makes it clear beyond all doubt that the sun, moon, and stars are the work of the creator and serve his purposes.[5]

The words "Let there be . . ." echo throughout this text. In that sense, "reason," out of which speech comes as expression, lies behind the universe envisaged by P. This leads Ratzinger to affirm: "Out of that 'Let there be' it was not some haphazard stew that was concocted. The more we know of the universe the more profoundly we are struck by a Reason whose ways we can only contemplate with astonishment. In pursuing them we can see anew that creating Intelligence to whom we owe our own reason."[6] This Reason is quite literally *awesome* in the strict sense of that much-abused word, leading Ratzinger to cite the words of St. Bonaventure: "Whoever does not see here is blind. Whoever does not hear here is deaf. And whoever does not begin to adore here and to praise the creating Intelligence is dumb."[7]

The refrain "God saw that it was good" occurs six times in this priestly narrative affirming the goodness of creation coming from God. Then in Genesis 1:31 we read, "God saw everything that he had made, and it was very good." The words "very good" appear only after the creation of Man and Woman. This is the seventh occurrence of the refrain "God saw that it was good" and given that in Hebrew thought the number seven signals fullness or completion, without being sheerly anthropocentric the text is telling us that the creation of human beings, both male and female equally, is the high-point of God's creative activity.

5. Scheffczyk, *Creation and Providence*, 7.
6. Ratzinger, "*In the Beginning*," 23.
7. Ratzinger, "*In the Beginning*," 24.

Genesis 1:26–27, describing the creation of humankind, provides and expresses deeper insight into God's creative activity. "Then God said, 'Let us make humankind in our image, according to our likeness; and let them have dominion over the fish of the sea, and over the birds of the air, and over the cattle, and over all the wild animals of the earth, and over every creeping thing that creeps upon the earth.' So God created humankind in his image, in the image of God he created them, male and female he created them." Putting the insights here together we might reflect with theologian Zachary Hayes in his relational summary of the meaning of this passage. "Human beings are intimately interwoven with the rest of the created order. The role of humanity is to live in such a way that the loving creativity of God will become manifest within the created order through human relations with other humans and with the non-human world. The life-style of humans should reflect in the world the loving, creative care of God for all of creation."[8]

The priestly theologian's wise insight does not end with the creation of humankind. Rather, his vision of God creating seems to reach its climax with the symbolism of the seventh day in Genesis 2:13:

> Thus the heavens and the earth were finished, and all their multitude. And on the seventh day God finished the work that he had done, and he rested on the seventh day from all the work that he had done. So God blessed the seventh day and hallowed it, because on it God rested from all the work that he had done in creation.

From the priestly author or source we may see here a legitimation of the Jewish practice of the Sabbath. This roots worship in the creation, after the creation of humankind. "Creation is designed in such a way that it is oriented to worship. It fulfills its purpose and assumes its significance when it is lived, ever new, with a view to worship. Creation exists for the sake of worship. . . . The Bible declares that creation has its structure in the Sabbath ordinance."[9]

---

8. Hayes, *Gift of Being*, 26.
9. Ratzinger, *"In the Beginning . . . ,"* 27–29.

God's good creation is to be celebrated in the prayer and praise of the Sabbath Day. It does not seem an exaggeration to say that *all* creation, and not only humanity, finds its *raison d'être* in adoration, the recognition of God, being "wowed" by God. In this vein systematic theologian Simon Oliver writes: "The liturgical cycle of worship is part of the created order. This implies that the fundamental orientation is towards the praise of God through a share in his life."[10]

Closely associated with adoration, I would say almost identical with it, is "praise." You cannot be aware of God's presence in adoration without feeling the need to praise him. The renowned Old Testament scholar Walter Brueggemann describes praise like this:

> Praise articulates and embodies our capacity to yield, submit, and abandon ourselves in trust and gratitude to the One whose we are. Praise is not only a human requirement and a human need, it is also a human delight. We have a resilient hunger to move beyond self, to return our energy and worth to the One from whom it has been granted. In our return to that One, we find our deepest joy.[11]

Praise is an attempt to cope with the sheer abundance of God's love, with we might say being "overwhelmed" by God. I don't think this adoration or praise of God is always entirely conscious as such. I recall, for example, sitting with a friend, someone who is not religious, watching a glorious sunset at the Oregon coast. The immense beauty of the sunset elicited from my friend the sentiment "I could watch this forever." Without wishing to impose my understanding on my friend's experience I would suggest that his experience might be described as "anonymous adoration." Further, I would argue that without such experiences of (at least) anonymous adoration it is impossible to flourish as a human being.

---

10. Oliver, *Creation*, 2.
11. Brueggemann, *Israel's Praise*, 1.

The Yahwist Narrative of Creation: Genesis 2:4b–25

Here too it is important to read through the whole narrative of creation for yourself. This creation narrative reflects the Yahwist perspective. "In contrast to the cosmic creator in the first chapter of Genesis, in Genesis 2 and 3 Yahweh is more intimate: he addresses humanity, issues commands, and walks in the garden of Eden to be present in, rather than beyond, his creation."[12] The Yahwist theologian/editor/source in the Pentateuch has sometimes been billed as the Bible's "first theologian."[13] The name "Yahwist" stems from his use of the name "Yahweh" for God, rather than "Elohim." The traditions that form this source may well go back to the time of David and Solomon. The Yahwist's God is anthropomorphic, what we might describe as a very human God. So, in Genesis 3:8 we find God "walking in the garden at the time of the evening breeze." When it comes to the creation of humankind, Yahweh is like an artist fashioning a human from the clay: "Then the LORD God formed man (*adam*) from the dust (*adamah*) of the ground and breathed into his nostrils the breath of life; and the man became a living being" (Gen 2:7). "This is creation by work rather than creation by word. At the same time, the supremacy of God over his creation is no less than in Genesis 1."[14] It has been pointed out by Scottish theologian David Fergusson that "the second creation narrative is more anthropological in focus. There is a different ordering of events, with the first human being (Adam) created prior to the other creatures."[15]

Joseph Ratzinger contrasts these creation narratives of Genesis with the Babylonian myth of creation, the Enuma Elish, in stark terms.

---

12. Oliver, *Creation*, 21.

13. I am thinking especially of the book by Ellis, *The Yahwist: The Bible's First Theologian*.

14. McKenzie, *Dictionary of the Bible*, 159.

15. Fergusson, *Creation*, 3.

There it is said that the world was produced out of a struggle between opposing powers and that it assumed its form when Marduk, the god of light, appeared and split in two the body of the primordial dragon. From this sundered body heaven and earth came to be. Thus the firmament and the earth were produced from the sundered body of the dead dragon, but from its blood [the god] Marduk fashioned human beings. It is a foreboding picture of the world and of humankind that we encounter here: The world is a dragon's body, and human beings have dragon's blood in them. At the very origin of the world lurks something sinister, and in the deepest part of humankind there lies something rebellious, demonic and evil. . . . In the face of the fear of any of these demonic forces we are told that God alone, who is the eternal Reason that is eternal love, created the world, and that it rests in his hands.[16]

The Genesis creation narratives are incomparably superior to the Enuma Elish.

The cosmogony of the ancient Near East and ancient Greece are laced with mythical motifs. As with the Enuma Elish, these cosmogonic myths point to a religious origin of the universe. The universe is not self-explanatory but owes its origin to some kind of "transcendent source." The creation narratives of the early chapters of Genesis, sometimes with points of contact with these mythical accounts, demythologize them, and propose God as the source of everything. While it must be admitted that the Genesis authors do not provide an account of creation as *creatio ex nihilo/creation out of nothing*, their theological understanding is certainly heading in that direction.

Perhaps we might say that the concern of the authors of the Genesis narratives of creation has more to do with the dependence of creation on God than on the beginnings of creation as such. God gifts creation. Creation comes from God as something gratuitously given. *How* it comes from God is not the central concern, but rather *that* it comes, and comes as gift. Returning to the epigraph of

---

16. Ratzinger, *"In the Beginning . . . ,"* 12–13.

David Fergusson at the head of this chapter, "Both creation stories in the early chapters of Genesis are *narratives of grace*. The making of the world in Genesis 1 is *a free and unconstrained act of God*."

Later theologians in the Christian tradition will coin the phrase *Bonum est diffusivum sui / Goodness is diffusive of itself*, "Goodness" meaning "God." Goodness/God does not wish to keep existence to himself, so to speak, but *passionately* wants to share existence with others, and so creation comes about. The Genesis authors do not know the phrase *Goodness is diffusive of itself* but they have intuited its meaning: generosity, gift-giving we may say, is the nature of God the Creator, and, therefore, generosity—gift-giving—is the grain of the universe.[17]

Creation in Deutero-Isaiah: Isaiah 40–55

The author whom scholars refer to as Deutero-Isaiah (Second Isaiah), the author of Isaiah chapters 40–55, is the poet laureate of the Old Testament. "A decisive breakthrough in the understanding and expression of Israel's faith in God as Creator came in . . . the amazingly rich thought of Second Isaiah."[18] The catastrophe of the Babylonian exile left Israel without king, temple, and land. The experience of exile became the catalyst for thinking and rethinking their theological traditions and also for the compilation of their sacred writings. This was the context for this extraordinary creative author about whom Elizabeth Johnson writes: "Proclaiming hope to a desperate people, the writing is magnificent, poetic, overflowing with beauty and assurance. Its basic message: have hope, because the infinitely good God who created heaven and earth is on the move to redeem you."[19] Let's read through Deutero-Isaiah's richly textured theological poems.

---

17. Some of these thoughts emerged from reading Anderson, "Creatio ex Nihilo and the Bible."
18. Butterworth, *Theology of Creation*, 28.
19. Johnson, *Creation and the Cross*, 31.

Isaiah 43:10–13

> Before me no god was formed,
>   nor shall there be any after me.
> I, I am the LORD,
>   and besides me there is no savior.
> I declared and saved and proclaimed,
>   when there was no strange god among you;
> and you are my witnesses, says the LORD.
>   I am God, and also henceforth I am He;
> there is no one who can deliver from my hand;
>   I work and who can hinder it?

Isaiah 44:24

> Thus says the LORD, your Redeemer,
>   who formed you in the womb:
> I am the LORD, who made all things,
>   who alone stretched out the heavens,
>   who by myself spread out the earth.

Isaiah 48:12–13

> Listen to me, O Jacob,
>   and Israel, whom I called:
> I am He; I am the first,
>   and I am the last.
> My hand laid the foundation of the earth,
>   and my right hand spread out the heavens.

In the midst of the powerful Babylonian pantheon—powerful not least because its gods, it was thought, had brought about the submission of Israel—this prophet, Deutero-Isaiah, asserts that there is only one God, and this one God is Israel's God, the creator of everything. Over against the magnificence of the annual Babylonian liturgy of creation, witnessed by the exiles, the God of Israel is the origin of everything and everyone, including the Babylonians.

"The biblical faith in God the Creator was thus largely a product of the experience of Old Testament writers who, under the inspiration of God himself, were able to expand Israel's faith in her *salvation* at the hands of God to the *creation* of all things at the hands of one and the same God. . . . Indeed, creation is only the first act in the historical drama of salvation."[20]

Staying with Deutero-Isaiah we also find creation itself praising God in Isaiah 49:13:

> Sing for joy, O heavens, and exult, O earth;
> break forth, O mountains, into singing!
> For the LORD has comforted his people
> and will have compassion on his suffering ones.

Creation here joins with the exiles in Babylon to praise God. If the exile in Babylon was the location, as seems to be the case, for the development of the synagogue, then in this beautiful text we see all creation joining the worshipers in the praise of God—the heavens, the earth, the mountains—all are singing. It is not at all fanciful to see the newly emergent synagogue as the place in which to sing God's praises. The Old Testament does not leave us with this magnificent cosmic theology of creation. There are indications throughout of God's personal care for the individual, and nowhere is this more evident than in some of the Psalms.

The Psalms

At this point it would be good to read through slowly Psalm 104. It is all about God's creative activity, verses 24 and 31 in particular

---

20. Butterworth, *Theology of Creation*, 43. Leo Scheffczyk notes in his *Creation and Providence*, 12: "Deutero-Isaiah is especially significant because of its affinity with the Priestly Creation narrative. Here, too, belief in creation historically justifies belief in redemption, so that Yahweh is recognized as both Redeemer and Creator (Isaiah 44:24). This soteriological interpretation of the concept of creation is most forcefully expressed in chapter 51, where the two works of creation coincide. Here God's deeds since the foundation of the world are linked to form a remarkable chain of saving events; not only is creation acknowledged as the primordial saving event but the history of the nation is described as a continuing act of God's creation."

summarize this activity. "O Lord, how manifold are your works! In wisdom you have made them all; the earth is full of your creatures.... May the glory of the Lord endure forever; may the Lord rejoice in his works." The final verse 35 does not at first glance seem to harmonize with this eulogy of God is the Creator—"Let sinners be consumed from the earth, and let the wicked be no more." One wonders what to make of this sentiment in a doxological poem of the Creator. Something similar occurs in Psalm 139:

1. O Lord, you have searched me and known me.
2. You know when I sit down and when I rise up;
    you discern my thoughts from far away.
3. You search out my path and my lying down,
    and are acquainted with all my ways.
4. Even before a word is on my tongue,
    O Lord, you know it completely.
5. You hem me in, behind and before,
    and lay your hand upon me.
6. Such knowledge is too wonderful for me;
    it is so high that I cannot attain it.
7. Where can I go from your spirit?
    Or where can I flee from your presence?
8. If I ascend to heaven, you are there;
    if I make my bed in Sheol, you are there.
9. If I take the wings of the morning
    and settle at the farthest limits of the sea,
10. even there your hand shall lead me,
    and your right hand shall hold me fast.
11. If I say, "Surely the darkness shall cover me
    and the light around me become night,"
12. even the darkness is not dark to you;
    the night is as bright as the day,
    for darkness is as light to you.

There is no place from which God is absent. One Old Testament scholar, Carroll Stuhlmueller, comments as follows: "For the psalmist to declare 'If I make my bed in Sheol,' is an open declaration that YHWH is also present in the abode of the dead. If YHWH abides there, then the spirits of deceased people are alive and at peace, they praise and thank God. . . . Psalm 139 therefore represents a break from the rigid orthodox position in the direction of popular or prophetic religious beliefs."[21] God's right hand holds him fast, protects him, leads him. It makes me think of George Herbert's wonderful line in his poem "Love III," "Love took my hand. . . ." A most moving image of God's creative and tender love for persons.

13. For it was you who formed my inward parts;
    you knit me together in my mother's womb.

14. I praise you, for I am fearfully and wonderfully made.
    Wonderful are your works; that I know very well.

15. My frame was not hidden from you,
    when I was being made in secret,
    intricately woven in the depths of the earth.

16. Your eyes beheld my unformed substance.
    In your book were written all the days that were formed for me,
    when none of them as yet existed.

17. How weighty to me are your thoughts, O God!
    How vast is the sum of them!

18. I try to count them—they are more than the sand;
    I come to the end—I am still with you.

"My inward parts" literally means in Hebrew "my kidneys." Every intimate part of me is shaped by God. God is like a skilled embroiderer, weaving me in secret. I am loved into being both by my parents and by God, the Ground of all being. "Conception is a most secret moment. Not only is intimacy between spouses wrapped in intimate secrecy, but the joining of ovum and semen takes place

---

21. Stuhlmueller, *Spirituality of the Psalms*, 136.

within the dark chambers of the new mother, unknown and uncertain to her and her spouse until many days later."[22] "I am loved into being." The understanding of creation in the Genesis narratives leads us to view creation as the generosity and gift-giving of God at work, literally a work of grace. This psalm puts existential clothing on this insight. It's not just the creation of the cosmos that is God's gift-giving, it's the human person, it's me!

Then, of course, we come to the disturbing verses of this psalm, disturbing in a way similar to Psalm 104:35.

19. O that you would kill the wicked, O God,
    and that the bloodthirsty would depart from me—
20. those who speak of you maliciously,
    and lift themselves up against you for evil!
21. Do I not hate those who hate you, O LORD?
    And do I not loathe those who rise up against you?
22. I hate them with perfect hatred;
    I count them my enemies.

Often these troubling verses are omitted in prayer ("castrated" in Roland E. Murphy's words) as unhelpful. "This seems wrongheaded. Should not prayer be realistic and confront human reality?"[23] Murphy is surely correct. The integrity of the entire text ought to be respected. At the same time, the difficult verses of 19–22 have to be dealt with. How ought we to do so, how ought we to understand these verses, to confront human reality, and, put more concretely, to confront *my* human reality? Three possibilities suggest themselves. *First*, recognize that the language is exaggerated, and should be understood as hyperbolic rather than as literal. *Second*, recognize the language as personifications of evil, rather than actual enemies, pointing to the spirit of revenge and violence lurking in my heart. *Third*, recognize that even at prayer we project our worst selves—our narrow tribalisms, our insularity, our exclusiveness—onto God. "The power of the Bible is largely that it gives

---

22. Stuhlmueller, *Spirituality of the Psalms*, 82.
23. Murphy, *Gift of the Psalms*, 168.

an unvarnished picture of human nature . . . and also of religion and the things that people do in its name."[24] Nonetheless, the final verses show that the psalmist is not complacent, "Search me!" He is aware of personal weakness.

> 23. Search me, O God, and know my heart;
>   test me and know my thoughts.
> 24. See if there is any wicked way in me,
>   and lead me in the way everlasting.

Probably the best known psalm in which all creation joins in the praise of God is Psalm 148. It would be good to open your Bible and read it through. If you do so, you would notice that the word "all" appears eight times in this psalm. *Everything created* is to join in this symphony of God's praise. One Scripture scholar actually describes Psalm 148 as "a cosmic choir of praise" or "a symphony orchestra," a most fitting description.[25] Picking up this theme of praise that runs throughout their book *Jubilate: Theology in Praise*, Daniel Hardy and David Ford emphasize that "creation's praise is not an extra, an addition to what it is, but the shining of its being, the overflowing significance it has in pointing to the Creator simply by being itself."[26] Clearly, Old Testament authors and especially the psalmist, had grasped the importance of creation praising the Creator, joining in chorus with all humankind.

Turning to the Wisdom Literature

"The notion of *hokmah* (wisdom) provides further evidence of the integration of creation and subsequent divine action in the Hebrew Bible. As the creative agency of God, wisdom is celebrated in the Psalms, Proverbs, Job, and in deutero-canonical works such as Sirach and the Wisdom of Solomon. . . . In some places, such

---

24. Collins, *Does the Bible Justify Violence?*, 31.
25. Bauckham, *Bible and Ecology*, 77–78.
26. Hardy and Ford, *Jubilate*, 83.

as Proverbs 8:12–36, wisdom is personified as a divine agent."[27] When we turn to the wisdom literature of the Old Testament, we find some interesting developments in the theology of creation. Take, for example, this fascinating passage from the book of Proverbs 8:22–31.

> The LORD created me at the beginning of his work,
>   the first of his acts of long ago.
> Ages ago I was set up,
>   at the first, before the beginning of the earth.
> When there were no depths I was brought forth,
>   when there were no springs abounding with water.
> Before the mountains had been shaped,
>   before the hills, I was brought forth—
> when he had not yet made earth and fields,
>   or the world's first bits of soil.
> When he established the heavens, I was there . . .
> When he marked out the foundations of the earth,
>   then I was beside him, like a master worker;
> and I was daily his delight,
>   rejoicing before him always,
> rejoicing in his inhabited world
>   and delighting in the human race.

"Wisdom" is being spoken of here in the highest possible terms. "Wisdom" is almost like a personification of the divine, and passages like this will be of central importance to the earliest Christian theologians as they seek to understand our Lord Jesus Christ. This passage is particularly fascinating, especially in the light of a comment from theologian Robert Butterworth: "To claim a special origin, prior to creation, from God, along with an active part in the divine work of creation, is to claim to be, in a way that was at this time by no means clear, equivalently divine, as God himself is divine, and yet somehow distinct from God. Later New Testament writers will see their way to being more precise about Wisdom's status, but for the present that status remains obscurely mysterious."[28] Wisdom's insight into creation blossoms into Chris-

---

27. Fergusson, *Creation*, 6.
28. Butterworth, *Theology of Creation*, 47.

tology, leading us to recognize the relationship between creation and the Christ, the creation narrative of the Easter Vigil leading to the account of the resurrection.

The book of Proverbs is not alone in this regard. The same basic thinking about Wisdom and creation is also found in the book of Ben Sira. In Ben Sira 24:3, 9 we read: "[Wisdom] came forth from the mouth of the Most High.... From eternity, in the beginning, he created me, and for eternity I shall not cease to exist." New Testament authors will call upon such passages concerning the figure of Wisdom to interpret the meaning of Jesus Christ. In Butterworth's words: "The figure of Wisdom, of divine status and with a special function with regard to God's creation as a whole, mysteriously born of God himself, and active in God's own creative activity, was seen to fit with what the first Christians came to realize, in faith, about Jesus Christ and about his relationship to all that existed."[29]

Conclusion

A constant concern for me in recent years is the disappearance of the Old Testament from systematic theology. Some, perhaps much contemporary systematic theology seeks to engage philosophy in its desire to make Christian faith more intelligent and persuasive to today's Christians. This is a praiseworthy objective. The Old Testament stands in traditional Christian faith as *necessary* to God's self-revelation. That is why chapter four of Vatican II's "Constitution on Divine Revelation" is entitled "The Old Testament." To neglect the Old Testament is to neglect God, and to neglect what the Old Testament authors have to say about creation makes the Christian tradition unintelligible.

---

29. Butterworth, *Theology of Creation*, 49.

3

Creation in the New Testament

> We Christians do not read the Old Testament for its own sake but always with Christ and through Christ.... We read it with him in whom all things have been fulfilled and in whom all its validity and truth are revealed.
>
> Joseph Ratzinger[1]

> The Hebrew notion of hokmah (wisdom) was later fused with the Greek concept of logos (word or reason) and became vital for expressing the linking of creation and Christology in the New Testament.
>
> David Fergusson[2]

> It is life itself which mediates the living knowledge of God for us, and a first principle of sacramental theology today is that it is the world, the human world, which is the basic sacrament, that is, the basic medium for making visible and for embodying the desire of the Father to give himself to beings other than himself. We have become accustomed to speaking of Christ as the sacrament of God in this sense. But since "in Christ all things were created" (cf. Col. 1:16), from the very creation of the world everything and above

---

1. Ratzinger, "In the Beginning...," 16.
2. Fergusson, *Creation*, 7.

> all the human, personal world exists in the Word, is already in Christ.
>
> Joseph Laishley[3]

Introduction

OUR INTRODUCTORY CITATIONS ARE making very important points about the contribution of the New Testament to the theology of creation. Joseph Ratzinger without in any sense denigrating the significance of the theology of creation in the Old Testament reminds Christians that both Testaments belong intrinsically together. Not only that, but Christians see the event of our Lord Jesus Christ as the climax, the filling-full of the meaning of the Old Testament. We read the books of the Old Testament for their own sake, yes, but we read them finally around the person of Christ. The theology of creation, then, is to be understood around the person of Jesus Christ. Creation and Christology belong inextricably together. The words of David Fergusson at the head of the chapter help us to realize that the connection between creation and Christ is forged through the Hebrew understanding of Wisdom now in alliance with the Greek concept of Logos/Word/Reason. Finally, the late English Jesuit theologian Joseph Laishley reenforces the connection of creation with Christ, of creation with Christology. The creation-Christology axis finds its most explicit articulation in the New Testament in both Pauline and Johannine theology.

Pauline Theology

Creation gets more attention in the letters of St. Paul than in the Gospels. Biblical scholar John L. McKenzie offers us a crisp summary of the core message of Paul about creation. "Paul makes Christ the principle of creation, the firstborn of every creature, in whom everything in heaven and earth is created, both visible and invisible. All things are created through him and tend to him.

---

3. Laishley, "Redemptive Love," 87.

Everything comes into being through him (Col. 1:15–20)."[4] Here is the complete text from Colossians:

> He is the image of the invisible God, the firstborn of all creation; for in him all things in heaven and on earth were created, things visible and invisible, whether thrones or dominions or rulers or powers—all things have been created through him and for him. He himself is before all things, and in him all things hold together. He is the head of the body, the church; he is the beginning, the firstborn from the dead, so that he might come to have first place in everything. For in him all the fullness of God was pleased to dwell, and through him God was pleased to reconcile to himself all things, whether on earth or in heaven, making peace through the blood of his cross.

Reading this fascinating passage closely, paying special attention to the prepositions used throughout—*in* him (Christ), *through* him, *for* him—leads us to the conclusion that Christ is not to be reduced to the historical Jesus, and further and more importantly, that Christ is not extrinsic to creation. Using language flowing from passages in the wisdom literature the earliest Christian theologians like St. Paul reached into the *nexus* between creation and Christ. "In fact, we might say that God's creative action reaches a high point in the relation between world and God in the one whom Christians call the Christ."[5]

We are so used in theological reflection to distinguish Christ from creation that that distinction becomes a separation, and no separation is allowed by this Pauline text. Distinction of Christ from creation, but without separation, receives a fine comment from Zachary Hayes when he says: "We might conclude from such texts, that the figure of Christ is not extrinsic to the universe. In fact, we might say that God's creative action reaches a high point in the relation between the world and God in the one whom Christians call the Christ."[6] Thinking along these lines is a powerful reminder

---

4. McKenzie, *Dictionary of the Bible*, 160.
5. Hayes, *Gift of Being*, 36.
6. Hayes, *Gift of Being*, 36.

that the incarnation was not a second thought on God's part, so to speak, in view of human sin and the need for redemption, but that the Christ was always "coming" to lead God's gift of creation to the highest possible plane, that is to say, consummation in God.

Johannine Theology

A note similar to St. Paul's theology of creation is found in the Gospel of St. John. In the Prologue (John 1:1–3) we read: "In the beginning was the Word, and the Word was with God, and the Word was God. He was in the beginning with God. All things came into being through him, and without him not one thing came into being."

John's text in Greek begins with the words *en arche / in the beginning*, immediately reminding the attentive reader of the exact same words found in the Septuagint Greek translation of Genesis, *en arche*. "Could it be that John is rewriting the opening of Genesis in the light of the Christian experience of Jesus Christ? Creation is a movement from chaos to cosmos, and the order that is characteristic of the cosmos is mediated through the eternal Word of God who became man fleshed in Jesus of Nazareth."[7] Words express something of the one who utters them. We may say that words, plural form of the noun, are the partial self-expression of the author. The plural "words" is not to be found in the Johannine Prologue, just the singular "Word." If God is manifested, partially self-expressed in all the various elements and entities of creation, the Word that is the Christ, the Word made human as Jesus, is the "full self-expression" of God. "God is free to express completely in Jesus who God is."[8] Again, the creation-Christology axis is emphasized in this Johannine text.

In the book of Revelation we read: "I am the Alpha and the Omega, the first and the last, the beginning and the end" (Rev 22:13). It is an astonishingly beautiful text. *Alpha* is the first letter

---

7. Hayes, *Gift of Being*, 37.
8. Ford, *Gospel of John*, 29.

of the Greek alphabet, and *Omega* is the last letter. This means not only that the whole of creation has its beginning in Christ, *Alpha*, but also finds its culmination and completion in Christ, *Omega*. Later we shall see this ancient Christian creation-Christology link waxed eloquently, for example, in the thought of Teilhard de Chardin.

The creation-Christological vision found in Paul and John is thrilling. Creation, in all its vastness, from the very first moment comes to be through Christ—the Eternal Word of God—and will reach its climax in Christ at the end. Reading especially from Pauline texts theologian Robert Butterworth has captured this vision nicely when he says, "This eternal Christ represents God's whole plan, God's entire purpose, what God eternally wills to accomplish and effect through his action in the world. . . . Christ is precisely that which God has eternally in mind. Christ is what God primarily and eternally wills."[9] While Christian theology sees creation as the consequence of God's free act, and in that sense as distinct from God, because creation is *in* and *through* the Eternal Word/Christ, it must be understood Christologically and never as separate from him, however challenging this might be to express.

Taking the Creation-Christological Vision Further

If we move to 1 John 4:16, where God is described as Love/*agape*—"God is love, and those who abide in love abide in God, and God abides in them"—then we can see creation as flowing from the Love that is God. This conviction was to perdure throughout the Christian tradition. A little-known author, D. J. Ehr, in an article in the *New Catholic Encyclopedia*, puts it splendidly:

> To believe in creation is to see Someone behind all things. It is to explain things themselves from an inner view—it is to see the world as a gift. . . . To create is above all to love. . . . To know that God creates man is to know at that point that man does not have to be loveable to be loved. To know man is created is to know that man is loved by

9. Butterworth, *Theology of Creation*, 58.

a love whose gratuitousness surpasses the most beautiful of human actions. In believing in creation man dares to affirm that all things rest on a "heart." The Old Testament tells us about the liberality of the Creator of the world; and St. John characterizes Him simply: He is love.[10]

And the Love that is God is fully expressed in the Word made human, in Jesus of Nazareth.

The Letter to the Hebrews

The Epistle to the Hebrews is most often associated with its theology of Christ the high priest, and that is undoubtedly its central concern. However, the term "high priest" is not so common in the early chapters of Hebrews. What is found in the first four chapters is a series of references that have to do with creation (Heb 1:2–3, 10–12; 2:5–10; 3:1–6; 4:3–4, 9–10).[11] At the very beginning of the Letter to the Hebrews (1:1–3) we read these words:

> Long ago God spoke to our ancestors in many and various ways by the prophets, but in these last days he has spoken to us by a Son whom he appointed heir of all things, through whom he also created the worlds. He is the reflection of God's glory and the exact imprint of God's very being, and he sustains all things by his powerful word.

Just like the passage from the Letter to the Colossians and the Prologue to St. John's Gospel the passage tells us of the cosmic role of Christ in creation. Christ is the one through whom God brought creation into being, and this same Christ sustains creation in being. This very clear affirmation of the cosmic role of Christ leads the historian of dogma Leo Scheffczyk rightly to conclude that "it

---

10. Ehr, "Creation," 420–22.
11. For a detailed analysis of this creation theme see Costley, *Creation and Christ*.

is therefore true to say that the idea of Christ's part in creation finds its most definite expression in the Epistle to the Hebrews."[12]

The Forest and the Trees

The student of Christian theology normally studies Christian doctrine in some kind of sequential form: the doctrine of the Triune God, Christology, pneumatology (the Holy Spirit), creation, ecclesiology, sacramental theology, and so forth. The richness of the tradition demands careful attention to these discrete aspects of Christian doctrine. The various disciplines of Christian theology may be likened to the individual trees in the Christian forest. At the same time, it is no less important to view the forest in its entirety, as it were, and attend not only to the individual trees. This is where the creation-Christology axis is so important. It helps us and encourages us to see the divine forest.

With this vision of the divine forest as well as the individual doctrinal trees, within the scope of the Scriptures from the beginning in Genesis to the end in the Apocalypse, David Fergusson provides us with a description of the whole:

> The doctrine of the person of Jesus Christ, as it develops already within the New Testament, is determined in important ways by the Hebrew account of creation. As the Word of God, he is identified with the creative agency celebrated throughout the wisdom literature. And the defeat of evil in the Apocalypse at the end of the Bible echoes the creation of the world from the waters of the deep in Genesis 1.[13]

This thrilling Christian panoramic vision leads us to cry out in praise of God, "How great Thou art!"

---

12. Scheffczyk, *Creation and Providence*, 28–29.
13. Fergusson, *Creation*, 2.

4

Creation in the Christian Tradition
The Patristic and Medieval Periods

> *By the end of the second century, the doctrine of creation out of nothing had emerged as the standard teaching of the church. The sudden and subsequent unanimity of support for this doctrine is one of the most interesting episodes in the history of dogma.*
>
> David Fergusson[1]

Introduction

LOOKING INTO THE CHRISTIAN theology of creation in the post-New Testament period, we see two bodies of traditions and texts, the scriptural texts known as the Old and New Testaments and the texts emanating from Greek philosophy. It has often been the case that theologians have made a too sharp contrast between these two sources of reflection, with "creation out of nothing" coming from Scripture and creation as some kind of "emanation" flowing from Greek philosophy. Contrast there certainly is, but an absolute

---
1. Fergusson, *Creation*, 15.

contrast between the two points of view is impossible. The intercourse and exchange between different cultures and world-views in antiquity is simply a matter of fact. People and cultures mingled and influenced one another. Accepting that introductory cautionary remark, let us now proceed to examine the issues in a little more detail.

Greek Philosophy

The major players, although not the only ones, in the early centuries of Christianity were Plato and Aristotle. The dialogue of Plato known as the *Timaeus* contrasts with the philosophy of Aristotle, and both of them were to exercise a singular influence on the Christian tradition of thinking about creation. Plato describes the creation of the world, the cosmos, from chaotic material by the divine craftsman known as the Demiurge. Aristotle's approach was quite different. For him the universe has always existed and so is eternal. These two thinkers, among others, form the constant backdrop to early Christian thinking about creation.

If we begin with Melissus of Samos (ca. 470–ca. 430 BCE), an early Greek philosopher and a contemporary of the post-exilic Jewish communities in Palestine, we find that he came to the conclusion in his reflections on nature that "nothing comes from nothing." If, in fact, nothing comes from nothing, and yet the something of this world exists, the question arises, "How are we to understand this?" The Greek philosophers who came after Melissus proposed various ideas. One of their ideas was that the world was eternal, and that came to be the point of view of the great Aristotle. Given the understanding of creation found in the first chapters of the book of Genesis, the notion that creation was eternal was unacceptable. That leads David Fergusson to affirm that "it is not until theologians contested the prevailing Greek philosophical assumption about the eternity of matter that the idea of creation out of nothing emerges as an articulated concept, albeit one that is presented as the most faithful to wider scriptural assumptions about the character of God and the dependence of the world."[2]

The Platonic belief that the world came to be through the organization of preexistent matter through the agency of the Demiurge was the basic alternative to Aristotle's view and became the position that was widely accepted in the Greco-Roman world. Following Plato's view in the dialogue known as the *Timaeus*, "the creator's work is to impose order upon a disorderly and recalcitrant matter. 'God therefore, wishing that all things should be good, and as far as possible nothing be imperfect, and finding the visible universe in a state not of rest but of inharmonious and disorderly motion, reduced it to order from disorder, as he judged that order was in every way better.'"[3] Matter was discordant and disorderly. The function of the deity was to produce order from this disorder. Alongside Platonism was the immensely popular philosophy of Stoicism and these two philosophies often intermingled in the popular mind. As Christianity began to emerge from the world of Judaism into the wider Greco-Roman world, it encountered this spectrum of philosophical ideas and positions.

Early Christian Theology

The second century saw the emergence of a group of Christian thinkers now known as the apologists, and their concern was to show the reasonableness of Christian faith in accord with some of the criteria of current philosophy, and also to dispel the myths that had been associated with Christians, such as incest and cannibalism. One of the earliest of these apologists was Aristides of Athens (dates unclear, but second century AD). An Athenian Christian thinker, Aristides of Athens, composed an *Apology for the Christian Faith*, only fragments of which still exist, but the fundamentals of his thought are clear. "It is noteworthy that Aristides, one of the earliest Apologists of the second century, opens his first

---

2. Fergusson, *Creation*, 16.
3. Fergusson, *Creation*, 17, citing Plato's *Timaeus* 30A.

chapter with arguments of natural philosophy, in the manner of Middle Platonism and the Stoa, to prove that an eternal, uncreated Being governs the universe and ensures its harmony (I, 1)."[4] Christianity is emerging into and engaging with the world of Hellenic philosophy. Aristides, influenced by the various currents of Greek philosophy of his time, essentially argues from the observable harmony of the universe to the existence of a Prime Mover, and this is God. God is responsible not only for the creation of the world but also for sustaining it. John N. D. Kelly, the magisterial doyen of early Christian theology, provides us with a pithy summary of how Aristides understands creation.

> The consideration of the order and beauty of the universe induced him to believe in a supreme Being who was the prime mover and who, remaining himself invisible, dwelt in his creation. The fact that there was a cosmos demanded a divine craftsman to organize it. Sovereign and Lord, he has created everything for man; reality came to be out of nothing at the behest of him who is incorruptible, unchanging and invisible.... The heavens do not contain him (here we may detect a criticism of Stoic pantheism, with its identification of God and the world); on the contrary, he contains them, as he contains everything visible and invisible.[5]

In this summary gathered and synthesized from what fragments of Aristides are available, Kelly demonstrates some key elements of Christian thinking about God and creation: the transcendence and immanence of God, God's creation "out of nothing," although there are echoes of the Platonic demiurge ordering reality from preexistent matter.

Aristides and apologetic thinkers like him—for example, Justin, Theophilus, Tatian—use terms for God derived from Platonic and Stoic philosophy. Such philosophic terms include *technites* (craftsman), *demiourgos* (demiurge), *despotes* (master), *pater panton* (father of all), *pater ton holon* (father of the whole). All of these

4. Scheffczyk, *Creation and Providence*, 56.
5. Kelly, *Early Christian Doctrines*, 84.

terms clearly point to God as the architect of creation but they fail to connect for the most part with a more scriptural understanding of God. The primary reason for this failure is the apologists' desire to establish connections with the regnant Greco-Roman philosophies. We do not find in these early Christian thinkers a connection with the creation-Christological perspective of the prologue to St. John's Gospel or the Letter to the Colossians. Philosophic considerations have the upper hand.

Moving into Patristic Theology

As we move on from the second-century apologists we find patristic authors engaged not only with alternative philosophies but much more fully with the Scriptures. The patristic theologian and specialist Paul M. Blowers has made a detailed and thorough study of creation in early Christian theology and he provides us with a summary account of patristic thinkers on creation. "Apologists, preachers and theologians throughout the early Christian age readily acknowledged the primary and critical importance of the 'Hexaemeron,' the six-day creation story (Gen. 1:1—2:4a), and of Genesis 1–3 as a whole, for developing normative Christian teaching about divine creation of the world."[6] Not only now do patristic theologians proceed from the Genesis accounts of creation, but also, noting the insights of the New Testament authors Sts. Paul and John, they equally see creation in Christological terms. The theological axis creation-Christ is beginning to manifest itself more clearly.

As the tradition developed, Blowers points out how these early Christian thinkers read the Bible as a whole, "Like a massive prophetic kaleidoscope, texts from across the Bible divulged different insights into the Creator's *oikonomia* [household management], his ongoing strategy to preserve, redeem, and perfect his creation."[7] Recognizing the absolute centrality of Christ,

---

6. Blowers, "Creation," 513. Blowers has a much fuller presentation of early Christian thinking about creation in his *Drama of the Divine Economy*.

7. Blowers, "Creation," 518.

these early Christians refused to separate creation from Christ as they read the Scriptures. St. Augustine, for example, combed the Psalms, interpreting them as Christocentric prophecy, viewing creation within the larger mystery of Christ, the church, and the new creation begun in Christ.

Marcionism, Gnosticism, Manichaeism

Christian thinkers also had to respond to other currents of thought that were proving attractive, currents of thought mainly negative in their appreciation of creation, and three in particular—Marcionism, Gnosticism, and Manichaeism.

Alternative accounts of creation emerged in Marcionism, Gnosticism and Manichaeism. Marcionites, following their leader Marcion (who died about AD 160), represented a real danger to developing Christian faith. This focused on his complete rejection of the Old Testament, as well as much of the New Testament. Whatever smacked of Jewish influence was to be abandoned. For Marcion, the Jewish creator God was a God of harshness and cruelty. This creator God was some kind of lesser deity, and certainly not the Father of our Lord Jesus Christ. The Jewish creator God, responsible, as Genesis affirmed, for the creation of the world, and so of the evil of matter, could have nothing to do with the God of love, the Father of Jesus.[8]

"Gnosticism" is a complicated phenomenon, but generally speaking it refers to a religious movement that claimed that salvation was based on secret knowledge (*gnosis*), and this secret knowledge was given to the elect by a heavenly revealer.[9] The movement flourished especially between the second and fourth Christian centuries, and presented an exceptionally strong

---

8. A useful summary of Marcionism may be found in Tilby, "Marcionism." In greater detail one might also consider H. Clifton Ward, "Marcion and His Critics."

9. For a balanced account of Gnosticism one might consult Bergquist, "Gnosticism."

challenge to the church—"Christianity was now fighting for its life."[10] Salvation for the Gnostic elect/chosen ones consisted of the ascent of the soul to a divine realm beyond the confines of this changing material world.

> The Valentinians (Valentinus was probably the most speculative of the Gnostic theologians) had spoken of creation as an emanation from the divine being. While not insisting upon the eternity of matter, this position represents the world as emerging from the nature of the divine self, although we should be aware that there is no one standard Gnostic account. Myths of emanation seem to presuppose gradations of being that flow downwards from God.[11]

The changing material world came from a malicious deity and was inherently evil. The challenge was to escape from the evil world by following the secret teaching of the divine revealer.

> In their polemics against Gnosticism, both Irenaeus and Tertullian reinforce and extend the doctrine of creation out of nothing. It is required not only to contest the assumption about the eternity of matter, but also to maintain the strict ontological distinction between the one God and all created reality. The cosmos does not represent a series of ontological gradations emanating from the divine outwards. There is one God, and everything else exists through the power of the Word of God.[12]

In the theology of St. Irenaeus of Lyons, in his treatise *Against the Heresies*, we find a robust response to Gnosticism.

> Creation is interpreted as a blessing from God, so that a link with redemption is already suggested. This link becomes explicit when the Creator and the Redeemer are identified with the person of Christ: the Son, or the Word in which all things were created, is recognized as Jesus the Redeemer. . . . If creation leads so inexorably

---

10. Scheffczyk, *Creation and Providence*, 68.
11. Fergusson, *Creation*, 18.
12. Fergusson, *Creation*, 19.

to redemption, then the latter must be its maturity and perfection. Hence this conception also implies growth: like man, the world, once created, has set out on a road that leads through the Incarnation and redemption to a more perfect fulfilment.[13]

Irenaeus has absorbed and expressed an understanding from the Scriptures, an understanding that is not only free of the metaphysical subtleties and speculations of Gnosticism, but also establishes the primacy of Scripture over the free-ranging intellect. Leo Scheffczyk comments further, taking the Irenaean perspective on creation to the celebration of the Eucharist.

> Creation also figures prominently in Irenaeus' conception of the Eucharist. Whereas many of the fathers regard the Eucharist as continuing the Incarnation, he sees it as continuing creation, because Christ's word turns the earthly gifts into food for men's souls, giving them a share in the life of the incarnate Son of God. Consequently he says it is a gross contradiction for the Gnostics to associate the earthly elements of bread and wine with Christ when they recognize not him but an alien, inferior demiurge as the creator of these elements.[14]

Manichaeism developed from the teaching of Mani (ca. 216–ca. 276), a native of Persia. At the core of his teachings was an absolute dualism, a total conflict between good and evil, between light and darkness. There is a family resemblance between Manichaeism and Gnosticism. In both, creation is not good. It is the arena of conflict between light and darkness, between the principles of good and evil in the universe. The goodness of creation, an idea flowing from the Genesis accounts, is simply mistaken. "Manichaeism offers a sophisticated dualist cosmology and anthropology not dissimilar to earlier forms of Gnosticism. The cosmos is the site of warfare between the material forces of good and evil.

---

13. Scheffczyk, *Creation and Providence*, 70–71.
14. Scheffczyk, *Creation and Providence*, 72.

Human beings with their moral struggles and mixed record are a microcosm of this."[15]

Moreover, as they encountered these alternative theologies of the Gnostics, Marcionites, and Manichaeans, early Christians tended to emphasize both the goodness of creation and also the continuities between creation and redemption in God's acting. "The overwhelming inclination of patristic exegesis was to confirm that the 'new creation', while greater than the original, was not its displacement but its elevation and transfiguration."[16] The Old Testament and the New Testament must be held together, even as we see the latter "filling-full" the former.

St. Augustine

"It was left to St. Augustine to give Western thought on creation its fullest and most definite form. His work fused the traditions of East (Basil, Gregory of Nyssa) and West in a new whole astonishing for its richness and intellectual depth."[17] Augustine was steeped in the philosophy of Plato, and he had also been for a time a Manichaean on his way toward Christian baptism by St. Ambrose of Milan. His understanding of creation may be seen "as a synthesis of, now as a defense against, those two schools of thought."[18]

From the Platonic tradition, and especially from Plotinus, Augustine calls God the "highest essence" (*On the Trinity* III.9.16), the primordial Good (*On the Trinity* VIII.3.4) and it is from God thus understood that all other being and goodness exists as a participation. He views creation reaching down in a kind of scale from the supreme reality of God to nothingness, the formless matter of the first chapter of Genesis. Furthermore, this action of God in creating is an action of God as Trinity. The relationality of the Trinity—three persons in communion—gives to all created

---

15. Fergusson, *Creation*, 22.
16. Blowers, "Creation," 522.
17. Scheffczyk, *Creation and Providence*, 97.
18. Scheffczyk, *Creation and Providence*, 97.

realities as certain Trinitarian structure or stamp, called by Augustine *vestigium Trinitatis* "footprint of the Trinity" (*On the Trinity* IX.2.2; XIV.16.22). As God's being is communion, what one might call the divine relationality, three persons in one God, so creation coming from this relational God also has a relational character. The Trinitarian footprint is throughout all creation, reaching its high point in humankind. In an interesting passage in his book *The Gift of Being*, Zachary Hayes comments on this Trinitarian relationality in creation:

> By and large, it has been assumed that the subatomic particles are isolated and independent particles. Yet in the quark research being done at Fermilab near Chicago it seems that quarks are discerned only in groups. If quarks are really the end of the line in the search for the ultimate building blocks, this may mean that the so-called building blocks are not isolated monadic blocks but are relational complexes. This points to the possibility that the cosmos is really systems within systems all the way down, and all the way out. If this is the case, then it seems that created reality is through and through relational. With that in mind, we can recall the core insight of the traditional Trinitarian concept of God: namely, that the divine reality is intrinsically relational in character. It may well be, then, that Christian believers today can see the cosmos as grounded in and as reflecting the relational character of the Trinity.[19]

Hayes (and many other scholars also) is not so much developing an apologia for the Trinity as recognizing the quite superb and amazing consonance between contemporary research in physics and traditional Trinitarian doctrine. This is a notion that we shall return to in the chapter dealing with contemporary theologians on creation.

Against the thought world of the Manichaens, Augustine stresses that evil is not a substance that has being of its own. In point of fact, evil is a *lack* of being, a privation of being (*Confessions* III.7.12). The world is not a combat zone between the good

---

19. Hayes, *Gift of Creation*, 69.

God and an evil principle. Augustine is optimistic in that sense—creation, the world, is fundamentally good.

The first five hundred years or so of Christianity witnessed the development of theology with regard to the Trinity and Christology. Early Christian councils drew out the Trinitarian nature of God, Christ as one person with two natures divine and human, the divinity of the Holy Spirit. These issues reflect the struggle for clarity within the Christian communities. No such struggle seems to obtain with the theology of creation at this time. Nevertheless, Christian reflection on creation stands out in contrast with other points of view and not only with the errant perspectives of Marcionism, Gnosticism, and Manichaeism. Positive creation theology did take place. It is well summarized by Rowan Williams: "The belief that God created the world out of nothing was unquestionably a *distinctive* Jewish and Christian view in the late antique world. Other accounts of creation may ascribe to God the initiative in setting things in motion or imposing order on passive matter, but the notion of an absolute origin is not be found with anything like comparable clarity outside the Judeo-Christian environment."[20] Both before and after the Council of Nicaea (AD 325) Christian theologians, although influenced by the philosophy of Plato and to a lesser extent of Aristotle, established creation as the work of God who also redeems and saves. Creation, redemption, salvation go together, as catechumens realized when they were handed over the creed to be recited at baptism and to be known "by heart." The creeds begin with creation—"I believe in one God the Father almighty, maker of heaven and earth"—move on to speak of redemption and salvation—"I believe in one Lord Jesus Christ"—and end with consummation—"I look forward to the resurrection of the dead and the life of the world to come." "Creation and salvation," patristic scholar Paul Blowers rightly maintains, "thus hung seamlessly together in a grand meta-drama extending from the primeval history to the final consummation," or, we might say, from Genesis to Apocalypse.[21]

---

20. Williams, "On Being Creatures," 67.
21. Blowers, "Creation," 522.

As we approach the Middle Ages, the question emerges, "Why does anything exist?" Rooted in the holy Scriptures generally and in the creation-Christological nexus of the New Testament particularly, the Christian tradition insists on answering the question "Why does anything exist?" only in relation to the infinite generosity of God. "Nothing preexists the creation of the world in the metaphysical sense. There is being from nonbeing only by the act of God. But what this is must be explained not by the sheer will of God but by the divine nature of wisdom and love. The world thus reflects something of its maker. Despite their ontological difference, there is a coordination of creation and creator."[22] Medieval thinkers, building on the patristic synthesis set out to explore further the theology of creation.

St. Maximus the Confessor (ca. 580–662)

Maximus was a Greek theologian and prolific scholar who was born in Constantinople just about ten years before the great prophet of Islam, Muhammad.[23] After holding an important court position under the Emperor Heraclius, Maximus became a monk and then later Abbot of the monastery of Chrysopolis on the eastern shore of the Bosphorus, near Chalcedon. In 626 as a result of the Persian advance toward Constantinople, Maximus, like many other monks, fled to Crete, and then later, about 628, to Carthage in North Africa, where he remained until 645. His opposition to the heresy of Monothelitism (the belief that Christ has only one will) got him into difficulties with the authorities leading to his exile and eventual death. Among his many works one might single out his *Ambigua/Difficulties*, an exegetical work on the Cappadocian theologian Gregory of Nazianzus, and his *Mystagogia*, an interpretation of the Eucharist.[24] The description of Maximus offered

22. Fergusson, *Creation*, 25.

23. Some of these details are taken from Cummings, *Eucharistic Doctors*, 84–85.

24. Aidan Nichols, *Singing-Masters*, 150, helpfully points out further what *Ambigua* means in relation to Gregory of Nazianzus: "The Latin word

by Paul Blowers and Robert Wilken is striking and worth quoting at some length.

> Maximus the Confessor (580–662) lived, historically, and to some extent geographically, betwixt and between. Historically, he lived in the indefinite transition between "early" and "medieval" Christianity: after the downfall of the Western Roman Empire and the zenith of the Byzantine Christian Empire under Justinian, but before the schism of Byzantine and Roman Churches had reached the point of no return; after the crucial Councils of Nicaea (325), Constantinople (381), and Chalcedon (451), but before the age of the Ecumenical Councils had ended; after the most creative epoch in patristic thought, stretching from Origen to the Cappadocian Fathers and Augustine, but before the tendency toward theological scholasticism East or West had fully gained momentum.[25]

This historical and theological contextualization of Maximus provides the non-specialist theological reader with a splendid portrait of his times.

Central to Maximus's theology was that the purpose of creation was the incarnation of the Eternal Word, the Son of God, and consequently, the divinization of humankind. "The two doctrines of creation and Incarnation are for Maximus closely connected. He sees the Incarnation as the goal of creation, the end or purpose God had eternally in view in creating the world and, within the world, mankind."[26] This is a stupendous claim and, perhaps, not so easy for at least Western Christians to grasp. Trying to get our

---

ambiguum translates the Greek *aporia*, a difficulty or problem, so Maximus was not necessarily saying Gregory had written unclearly. He could be—and was—saying that Gregory had left some problems unresolved." For a brief understanding of Maximus on the Eucharist, see Cummings, *Eucharistic Doctors*, 85–92.

25. Maximus the Confessor, *On the Cosmic Mystery of Jesus Christ*, trans. Blowers and Wilken, 13. As well as the work of Blowers and Wilken, there is a very fine detailed and exegetical account of Maximus in Wood, *The Whole Mystery of Christ*.

26. Nichols, *Singing-Masters*, 149.

human minds around the utterly incomprehensible reality of the Triune God, of creation, of incarnation/redemption, of consummation/parousia/eschaton, is really impossible. For the purpose of some limited theological understanding of the Mystery we "break" it up into more intellectually digestible parts. What Maximus is doing with his theology of creation is reconfiguring our fragmentary, digestible, doctrinal parts into a divine whole, cumbersome though that language may appear to be. Although his synthesis is clearly his own, in reality it seems to me that he is retelling the Scriptural story as a unity. Scripture begins with God, with God creating through his word—his words in Genesis chapter 1. Those creating utterances of God are in fact one Word, the Eternal Word, whom we learn in St. John's Prologue and the first chapter of Ephesians and Colossians 1:15–23 is the divine medium through which everything came to be and who became one of us humans.[27] Through the entire Christ-event, the entire Word-event, centering in the death, resurrection, ascension, and gift of the divine Spirit, we are healed of our sinfulness, made whole and holy in Christ, and we are being led to the fullness of the Word's presence that we know as the parousia. The story begins in the book of Genesis and ends in the book of the Apocalypse. We might describe all of this as the classical Christian understanding of God-creation-incarnation. Returning to Aidan Nichols for a moment, he puts it like this:

> The reason we should want to say (all of the above, and especially affirming the human will of Jesus Christ) is not just metaphysical. More than that, it is soteriological. Unless the human nature of the incarnate Word had its own willing, its own agency, the humanity of Christ could not enjoy that *tropos*, that mode of existing and acting. And without that particular *tropos*, the Son could not change the condition of our humanity from within in the way that is required by the foundational principle of Christian soteriology, which states, in Gregory

---

[27]. Blowers and Wilken describe Maximus's vision as "a panoramic commentary" on the Pauline texts. See Maximus the Confessor, *On the Cosmic Mystery of Jesus Christ*, 20.

Nazianzen's words, "What has not been assumed has not been healed."[28]

Maximus's vision and achievement has been described as a grand "symphony of experience" rather than a perfectly contoured and self-enclosed system.[29]

In this grand symphony for Maximus the incarnation was not, so to speak, an "afterthought" on God's part. It was always God's thought, always God's plan, and, of course, by incarnation we necessarily include what we mean by "redemption." The Trinitarian reality of Father-Son-Spirit exploded through the Love that God is into being, into creation, and the highest moment or most intense expression of this Trinitarian explosion is the incarnation, leading ultimately to final consummation in the Trinity.

John Scotus Eriugena (ca. 810–77)

Following our treatment of Maximus the Confessor comes the philosopher and theologian known as John Scotus Eriugena, who, in point of fact, was the Latin translator of Maximus's *Ambigua*. Eriugena is much less known than later medieval thinkers. Scotus means "Irish," and Eriugena means "of Irish birth." Eriugena was an Irishman and a man of three cultures—Celtic, Latin, and Greek. His theology of creation places an emphasis on the immanence of God, and this emphasis leads Scottish theologian John Macquarrie to say of him, "It is tempting to speculate that Celtic spirituality, with its strong emphasis on the immanence of God in nature and in daily life, has to be reckoned along with Neo-Platonism as the source of Eriugena's later teaching about the manifestation of God in the things of this world."[30] It is unknown if Eriugena was a priest, a monk, or a layman. It is certain that he lived part of his life in Ireland at one of the well-established monasteries in which he would

---

28. Nichols, *Singing-Masters*, 159–60.

29. By Blowers and Wilken in Maximus the Confessor, *On the Cosmic Mystery of Jesus Christ*, 16, citing the Orthodox theologian George Florovsky.

30. Macquarrie, *In Search of Deity*, 85.

have begun his studies. Classical Old Irish words are to be found in his biblical glosses, thus showing him to be educated not only in Christian literature, but also in Irish literature. He was well-versed not only in Celtic literature but also in Latin and Greek authors. Thus, he translated the [Greek] writings of Pseudo-Dionysius the Areopagite and the *Ambigua* of Maximus the Confessor into Latin. His greatest work was the *Periphyseon* or the *De Divisione Naturae*, "On Nature," written between 860–66, and described by the historian of theology Bernard McGinn as "the first medieval summa, that is, a truly systematic account of all reality, or of nature."[31] It is here that we find his theology of creation.

For Eriugena, from God as Creator flows the differentiated creation, but in the end all things will return to God, he will cease to create and all things will be at rest in him. Nature is coextensive with reality. Nature should be divided into four categories. The first category is Nature which is not created but creates, that is, God. God as Creator cannot simply be part of the universe. "This is the absolutely undifferentiated primordial unity of God."[32] God is transcendent, utterly beyond human grasp. Second, is Nature which is created and which creates. This is the world of primordial causes or the Platonic ideas, and this second Nature proceeds from the first Nature. "It is the intelligible world, the world of essences, forming a unity in the Logos.... As a Christian... he identifies this second nature with the second Person of the Trinity."[33] Third, is Nature which is created and which does not create. These are the things perceived through the senses, and this proceeds from the second Nature. This being so, "Everything that exists... is a theophany, a manifestation of God. Even more, the reality of things is nothing

---

31. McGinn, *Growth of Mysticism*, 82.

32. Hawkins, *A Sketch of Medieval Philosophy*, 26. Hawkins (1906–64) was a Thomist priest-scholar whose interests engaged with British philosophy. Needless to say, his work on Eriugena has been eclipsed by the outstanding studies of (*inter alios*), Moran, *The Philosophy of John Scotus Eriugena*, and McGinn and Otten, *Eriugena, East and West*. Hawkins's sketch of Eriugena's thought remains valuable for its exceptional clarity of exposition.

33. Hawkins, *A Sketch of Medieval Philosophy*, 26.

other than the reality of God unfolding itself."[34] In Eriugena's own words: "It follows that we ought not to understand God and the creature as two things distinct from one another, but as one and the same. For both the creature, by subsisting, is in God; and God, by manifesting Himself, in a marvelous and ineffable manner creates Himself in the creature, the invisible making Himself visible and the incomprehensible comprehensible. . . . Eternal He begins to be, and immobile He moves into all things and becomes in all things all things."[35] It is theophany that makes speech about God possible. Fourth and finally, is Nature which neither creates nor is created, that is, God, to whom all things must in the end return. "Things fulfil their destiny not by perishing but by being taken up once again into the divine unity."[36] The four categories of Nature may be understood as the traditional *exitus* (exit/creation) of all things from God and the *reditus* (return) of all things to God, the Alpha and the Omega of the book of Revelation. In Eriugena's perspective, fundamentally God is all things everywhere but arguably not ending up in a crude pantheism. Rather, in the words of John Macquarrie, "Eriugena is making every effort to bring together transcendence and immanence, not in any weakening compromising form, but thoroughgoing transcendence together with complete immanence."[37]

The great French medievalist Étienne Gilson writes of Eriugena: "No one, after him, has ever dared to take up as a whole a doctrine so little suited to the sober teachings of the Latin tradition, but it was to remain as a sort of permanent temptation against which, from century to century, doctrinal authorities were never to cease struggling, without ever succeeding in killing it."[38] The permanent temptation was to side with transcendence over

---

34. Hawkins, *A Sketch of Medieval Philosophy*, 27.

35. *Periphyseon* 678C, cited in O'Meara, *Eriugena*, 305. O'Meara's own translation of *Periphyseon* is *Eriugena, Periphyseon*, translated by John J. O'Meara.

36. Hawkins, *A Sketch of Medieval Philosophy*, 27.

37. Macquarrie, *In Search of Deity*, 87.

38. Gilson, *History of Christian Philosophy in the Middle Ages*, 128.

immanence or with immanence over transcendence in respect of God and his presence in creation. Eriugena was a mystic, and so "we might expect then that Eriugena's mysticism would be in the last degree apophatic—since that is the mystical way—but not so. God is not simply distant and unknown but has descended into his creation and shown himself in theophanies."[39] It is impossibly difficult to hold these two principles of divine transcendence and divine immanence together, but Eriugena's attempt, to say the least, is not only commendable but provides an attractive theology of creation.

St. Thomas Aquinas (1225–74)

"[Aquinas's] work is a junction at which converge three roads: Greek philosophy in its Aristotelian and Neoplatonic guises; patristic theology of West and East; and, most importantly, of scripture."[40] When we enter the world of medieval theology, it is a world that we can recognize as continuous with the patristic world, but it is also a world marked by new challenges and new developments in theological thought. This is how it is described by Leo Scheffczyk: "Classical scholastic thought about creation must accordingly be seen as an attempted synthesis between the old Neoplatonist Augustinianism of tradition and the new Aristotelianism, a synthesis which took various forms in the various schools and types of theology—a sign of the luxuriant intellectual growth which the dogma of creation was undergoing."[41] If Eriugena is to be seen on the Neoplatonist side of the theological spectrum, St. Thomas Aquinas, while he has undoubtedly inherited important elements of Neoplatonism, is more decidedly and demonstrably Aristotelian in his thinking.[42]

---

39. Macquarrie, *Two Worlds Are Ours*, 111, slightly adapted.
40. This is how Simon Oliver introduces Aquinas in Oliver, *Creation*, xii.
41. Scheffczyk, *Creation and Providence*, 136.
42. Note, however, the important qualifying comment of Scheffczyk, *Creation and Providence*, 149: "Platonism never wholly disappeared from medieval philosophy, and it is present in Thomist thought about creation."

"For St. Thomas, creation is the reception of being from the giver of all existence. Creation is a relation to the creator as the fount of our being. God *is* being. He is the fullness and perfection of existence. All created beings *have* being. They have being as a participation in what God *is* fully and perfectly. This participation defines creaturehood."[43] This summary comes from the Irish systematic theologian Denis Carroll and offers us a terse but accurate account of Aquinas's theology of creation. Aquinas is restrained in pursuing the question of the origins of creation, as an act at the beginning of everything.

Aquinas is much more interested in emphasizing creation as the reception of existence from the One who is Being Itself. "Creation is nothing other than a relation to the Creator as the fount of our being."[44] His point of view may be understood in two ways: as active creation and as passive creation. As active, creation is to be understood as called forth not from any prior existing material but from nothing, the creative act of God. Continuing with Denis Carroll, "Creation is not an artifact. It is a gift, not of improved or altered being, that of being pure and simple."[45] As passive, creation is that which arises from the gift and reception of existence. Aquinas is searching for a more deeply ontological understanding of the dependence of creation upon God. He wants to understand why things actually exist and why they continue to be held in being. In the words of the celebrated Thomist theologian, Herbert McCabe, OP, "Every action in the world is an action of God; not because it is not an action of a creature but because it is by God's action that the creature is *itself* and has its *own* activity."[46] Aquinas's concern is not simply with how creation got started once upon a

---

43. Carroll, "Creation," 251. Carroll's article on creation anticipates his excellent book *Towards a Story of the Earth*. There are other scholars, specialists in the theology of Aquinas, to whom one might turn to explore more fully his theology of creation, for example, Wawrykow, "Aquinas and Bonaventure on Creation." My choice of Denis Carroll as guide for Aquinas arises from the clarity of his thought and his felicitous, contemporary style.

44. Carroll, *Towards a Story of the Earth*, 43.

45. Carroll, "Creation," 251.

46. McCabe, *God Matters*, 7.

time—active creation. Thus, his understanding of divine creation is closely allied to a strong sense of divine conservation or preservation—passive creation. "God not only creates but constantly holds everything in being in a single act of sustaining."[47] Putting these two ways of understanding creation together, active creation and passive creation, we might put it like this: for Aquinas, it is not the case that God is simply there, and then suddenly at the moment of creation we have God-plus-the universe, as it were. Everything exists by sharing in the existence of God.[48] Putting it humorously Carroll writes: "Creation, in this sense, is not a first 'kick-off'. It is not as if God were a clockmaker who, having set up the works and wound the springs, left the clock to itself until some repairs were needed."[49]

Thinking in terms of time is not particularly helpful here, as if to say something like "*before* being there was nothing." "Creation is not about the before and after. It is rather about an order of being—of reception from a total source."[50] An important consequence of this way of thinking is that one should attribute causality both totally to God and at the same time totally to creatures. Again, turning to Denis Carroll, "A good action, a beautiful gesture, comes from God as well as from the doer. Indeed, we can say of an evil action that it is permitted by God for he does not subtract his conserving force from the evildoer."[51] It is a magnificent vision. God's presence is there, in everything, in all human knowing and willing, even if it is not immediately recognized as such. As recognized, creation is understood as gratuitous gift. "God creates out of love. The motive of creation is a selfless love. And the most natural thrust in all creation is to return thanks for that creative, pre-existent love."[52]

---

47. Fergusson, *Creation*, 29.
48. See Oliver, *Creation*, 48.
49. Carroll, *Towards a Story of the Earth*, 45.
50. Carroll, "Creation," 251.
51. Carroll, "Creation," 252.
52. Carroll, *Towards a Story of the Earth*, 49.

How Great Thou Art

St. Francis of Assisi (ca. 1181–1226)

St. Thomas Aquinas was born one year before St. Francis of Assisi died. Church historian Kevin Madigan, drawing some parallels between the pursuit of the historical Jesus and that of the historical Francis, points out the challenges of reaching historical accuracy about Francis. As with the canonical Gospels we have various Christologies, ways of understanding the Lord Jesus, so with St. Francis. We have various "Franciscologies."[53] While Aquinas was the great systematic theologian, Francis was a poetic theologian. Tradition has it, in the Franciscology of Brother Leo, that on the evening of his death (October 3, 1226) St. Francis sang Psalm 141. The first two verses provide context and content:

> I call upon you, O Lord; come quickly to me;
> give ear to my voice when I call to you.
> Let my prayer be counted as incense before you,
> And the lifting up of my hands as an evening sacrifice.

His great Canticle of the Sun is his contribution to the theology of creation:

> Most High, all powerful, good Lord,
> Yours are the praises, the glory, the honor, and all blessing.
> To You alone, Most High, do they belong,
> and no man is worthy to mention Your name.
> Be praised, my Lord, through all your creatures,
> especially through my lord Brother Sun,
> who brings the day; and you give light through him.
> And he is beautiful and radiant in all his splendor!
> Of you, Most High, he bears the likeness.
> Praised be You, my Lord, through Sister Moon and the stars,
> in heaven you formed them clear and precious and beautiful.
> Praised be You, my Lord, through Brother Wind,
> and through the air, cloudy and serene,
> and every kind of weather through which you give sustenance
>   to Your creatures.
> Praised be You, my Lord, through Sister Water,
> which is very useful and humble and precious and chaste.

---

53. Madigan, *Medieval Christianity*, 227–28.

Praised be You, my Lord, through Brother Fire,
through whom you light the night and he is beautiful
and playful and robust and strong.
Praised be You, my Lord, through Sister Mother Earth,
who sustains us and governs us and who produces
varied fruits with colored flowers and herbs.
Praised be You, my Lord, through those who give pardon for Your love,
and bear infirmity and tribulation.
Blessed are those who endure in peace
for by You, Most High, they shall be crowned.
Praised be You, my Lord, through our Sister Bodily Death,
from whom no living man can escape.
Woe to those who die in mortal sin.
Blessed are those who will find Your most holy will,
for the second death shall do them no harm.
Praise and bless my Lord, and give Him thanks
and serve Him with great humility.[54]

As Francis hymns the praise of God he draws all creation, all creatures into this magnificent doxology. The sun, the moon, the stars, the weather, water and fire, mother earth, the flowers and the herbs—all creatures sing God's praises. Then, almost like the Priestly creation account in Genesis 1, St. Francis turns to humankind to praise God, even through bodily death. The medievalist Jacques Le Goff captures something of Francis's unique vision of creation when he compares the thought of Francis with the theological and ecclesial context of his day:

> In this world that was becoming one of exclusion imposed by the legislation of the councils and the decrees of canon law ... Francis proclaimed, without the slightest hint of pantheism, the divine presence in all creatures. Between the monastic world bathed in tears and the unconcerned masses sunk in an illusory gaiety, he placed the blissful laughing face of one who knows that God is joy.[55]

---

54. Armstrong et al., *Francis and Clare*, 37–39.
55. Le Goff, *Saint Francis of Assisi*, 11.

Even acknowledging the somewhat hyperbolic element in Le Goff's words they have the ring of truth about them, especially when he notes in Francis "without the slightest hint of pantheism, the divine presence in all creatures" occasioning God as Joy.

A contemporary Franciscan theologian, Kenan Osborne, endorses this point of view when he says:

> Francis realized that God loved our world and wanted to be with us. . . . Creation for him was a powerful, living mural of God's love. . . . One could easily say that God's presence in and through creation itself is a mini-incarnation and that God's presence in the humanness of Jesus is a maxi-incarnation. Both the presence of God in the created universe itself and the presence of God in Jesus are incarnationally inter-related. . . . The entire earth, just as it is, is a gospel of divine presence.[56]

Creation itself, we may say, is the very beginning of the incarnation. Here we find an echo of Maximus's vision. From today's vantage point in the twenty-first century the canticle has a profound resonance, weaving all reality together in a holistic fashion in a profound ecology of praise.

Dame Julian of Norwich

In one of her illness visions Julian is shown by God "something small, no bigger than a hazelnut, lying in the palm of my hand," and God explained to her that this hazelnut was in fact "everything which is made" (ST 4).[57] She wondered about the smallness of the nut, and how it could easily disappear, but it came to her mind that "it lasts and always will, because God loves it; and thus everything has being through the love of God" (ST 4). This is very sound and very traditional theology, going back ultimately to the affirmations of creation's goodness in the narrative of Genesis 1. There appear to be echoes here—not necessarily intentional but

---

56. Osborne, *The Franciscan Intellectual Tradition*, 36–37.

57. There are two versions of Julian's "Showings." The first version is called the Short Text (ST) and the much longer version the Long Text (LT).

absorbed through the popular Christian culture—of Pseudo-Dionysius and Aquinas, that the motive for creation is *Bonum est diffusivum sui*, "Goodness (God as Love) is diffusive of himself." Love is the motive for creation. At the same time, her affirmation that "it lasts and always will" points to the basic Christian conviction that creation will find its *telos* in God, that it is not destined for annihilation for consummation in God. This is an immensely positive theology of creation.

The positive theology of creation is taken further in her reflection when she continues that "God is everything that is good, and the goodness that is in everything is God" (ST 5). Now this is very strong language, language expressive of God's immanence in creation. It is what the Kerry philosopher-poet John Moriarty (1938–2007) is talking about when he describes "the universe as a shimmer of God within God."[58]

Conclusion

This chapter is not intended to provide a comprehensive or exhaustive survey of the history of Christian thought about creation. It is more of a creation "smorgasbord," highlighting some of the understandings of creation as the tradition developed. However, I think it is possible to see some common themes that have become important to Christian theology. These common themes include: God's transcendence of creation and also his immanence in creation; a growing Trinitarian awareness *vis-à-vis* creation; a concern to recognize the Christological connection, what I have called the "creation-Christological" axis; the sheer goodness of creation as gift-of-God; and finally, the ongoing conversation between philosophy and theology.

---

58. Moriarty, *Serious Sounds*, 9, 63.

5

Creation in the Christian Tradition

From the Renaissance to Pope Francis's *Laudato Si*

> *We may say it was Aristotle rather than Ptolemy who had to be overthrown in the sixteenth century. It was necessary to make a great advance on the general scientific teaching of Aristotle before the world could be in a position to do justice to the Copernican hypothesis.*
>
> Herbert Butterfield[1]
>
> *Science is as much the genesis of wonder as a claim to comprehension.*
>
> Frances M. Young[2]

IF HISTORIAN OF SCIENCE Herbert Butterfield implicitly tells the story of what happened to the relation between faith and science beginning in the sixteenth century, theologian Frances Young gives fine expression, at least for many contemporary scientists, of the centrality of wonder. The continually expanding wonder that drives science is of necessity open-ended. There is always more to be discovered in so many different ways. This, however, may

---

1. Butterfield, *Origins of Modern Science*, 36.
2. Young, *God's Presence*, 44.

be contrasted with "scientism," a closed point of view that will be commented on below.

The Renaissance

This opening statement of the historian of science, Herbert Butterfield, needs to be taken seriously. Butterfield points out in great detail how physics and philosophy had come to be predominant Aristotelian in the West and in Christianity through the influence especially of St. Thomas Aquinas. The cosmology of the Italian poet Dante Alighieri (ca. 1265–1321), for example, was based on Aristotelian thought. Butterfield says of Dante in this regard: "In [Dante's] whole picture of the universe there is more of Aristotle than of Christianity."[3] One might contest that judgment of Dante, but it certainly points to the towering presence of Aristotelian thought.

We must add to this wedding of Aristotelian philosophy to Christian revelation the cosmology of Ptolemy. Ptolemy (ca. 100–ca. 168 CE) was an astronomer and mathematician from the great Egyptian city of Alexandria, one of the greatest centers of learning in the ancient world. Around 150 CE he composed his *Almagest* and *Planetary Hypotheses*. Here we find his understanding of cosmology. The Ptolemaic system is a geocentric cosmology; that is, it assumes that the earth is stationary and that it is at the center of the universe, a system known as geocentrism, earth-centeredness. The sun revolved around the stationary earth. Born at the time when Christianity was moving out from Judaism into the wider Hellenistic world of thinking, if and when Christians thought about cosmology, they thought of it in Ptolemaic terms. Ptolemaic cosmology seemed to gel with biblical cosmology. Ptolemaic geocentric science persisted basically until the new science heralded by people like Nicholas Copernicus in the fifteenth and sixteenth centuries.

---

3. Butterfield, *Origins of Modern Science*, 35. While Butterfield's perspective concerning Aristotle remains true, it tends to overlook the lingering Platonic influence in Christian thinking. See, for example, Madigan, *Medieval Christianity*, 279–83.

This wedding of Aristotelian and Ptolemaic science to the theology of creation began to come apart with the Renaissance. The Renaissance is that period in history from the end of the Middle Ages and transitioning through the fifteenth and sixteenth centuries. It has been described in the following terms:

> Intellectual change expressed itself in an exaltation of man and his individuality, in a heightened critical sense (evident alike in historiography, medicine, and natural science), and in a new sense of space which stamped the age of geographical and astronomical discovery. The collapse of the geocentric universe and of the whole world picture familiar to antiquity and the Middle Ages, plunged man into a far vaster world, both physically and intellectually, and gave him, mind and will, a sense of power undreamed of before.[4]

Human understanding of the world and everything about it was changing and changing very fast. As knowledge of the world and the heavenly bodies expanded, it was inevitable that new knowledge would clash with the received biblical understanding of reality as well as the received but now outdated Ptolemaic cosmology. Unfortunately, theology did not develop along with the fast-changing understanding of reality but tended to remain content with a medieval view of the world and Ptolemaic cosmology. Consequently, a certain hostility began to develop between the church and science, so much so that Leo Scheffczyk comments that the Renaissance was "the first great intellectual movement which threatened Christian theism in the West to its very roots."[5] Other threatening intellectual movements were afoot in the reforming currents of the sixteenth century.

Galileo, Copernicus, Newton, Darwin

The hostility between the theology of creation and the emerging sciences began to take shape especially with the views of Nicholas

4. Scheffczyk, *Creation and Providence*, 173.
5. Scheffczyk, *Creation and Providence*, 174.

Copernicus (1473-1543) and Galileo Galilei (1564-1642). Both thinkers were foundational in the transition from a geocentric (Ptolemaic) universe to a heliocentric (Copernican) universe. Galileo was and always remained a devout Catholic, even as he tried to remain faithful to his scientific methodology. In 1543 the Polish lay canon and astronomer Copernicus asserted that the earth circled the sun, not the other way around, as had been traditionally thought. Copernicus dedicated his treatise *On the Revolutions of the Heavenly Spheres* to Pope Paul III. There was little or no immediate public reaction. However, in 1616 the Congregation of the Holy Office declared that the heliocentric hypothesis was heretical, and Galileo was convicted in 1633 of disobeying an injunction imposed upon him not to promulgate the ideas of Copernicus. He remained under house arrest until his death in 1642. The problem, as the church saw it at the time, was the seeming incompatibility between the traditional geocentrism (presupposed by both Scripture and the received Ptolemaic/Aristotelian view of physics) and the new Copernican worldview. In Scripture were to be found texts asserting that the earth was motionless and the sun was moving—for example, Joshua 10:12-13, Psalm 104:5, Ecclesiastes 1:5, and, of course, Scripture was inerrant. Not less inerrant, it was understood, was Aristotelian physics. Keith Ward writes: "The conflict was not so much between Christian faith and the Copernican view that the earth circles the sun, as between established Aristotelian science and the 'new science' of close observation and experiment that was threatening the old scientific elite."[6] Theology and empirically based science tended now to go their separate ways.

New developments were taking place throughout the entire Christian world, developments that would require appropriate

---

6. Ward, *Pascal's Fire*, 9. James P. Mackey adds a useful comment to Ward: "Rather were they [the disputes with Galileo and later with Darwin] disputes between, on the one hand, current establishment views representing that inextricable mixture of science and theology which has just been shown to be the norm in Western philosophy as a whole and, on the other hand, emerging views that, as part and parcel of the normal advance of knowledge, challenged some important part of the establishment view in each case." See his *The Scientist and the Theologian*, 26-27.

responses. For example, the discovery of the New World by Christopher Columbus in 1492 and other such discoveries led to a huge expanse of Christian missionary activity throughout the world. At another level, it is instructive to note that the reformer Martin Luther died just three years after the death of Copernicus in 1546. Developments were taking place not only geographically throughout the Christian world but also theologically within the Christian world. The challenges emerging from the new empirical approaches to science were to continue, and "the dominant operative model in dealing with science and theology was one of suspicion."[7]

Following in the wake, as it were, of Galileo and Copernicus came the English mathematician and scientist Isaac Newton (1643–1727). He published in 1687 *Mathematical Principles of Natural Philosophy*, in which he formulated the scientific laws of motion and gravitation, providing the foundations of physics for centuries to come. Turning again to theologian Keith Ward for comment: "The idea that nature operates in accordance with general laws, so regular and precise that they can be captured in mathematical equations, is astonishing and unexpected. For most of human history events in nature were widely believed to be caused by the actions of spirits, gods or demons. Their actions often seemed to be arbitrary, or contradictory."[8]

The scientific breakthroughs of Copernicus, Galileo, and Newton made it clear that the methodology of science is to seek a naturalistic explanation of events based on verified laws. The benefits to humankind that flowed from the new scientific thinking and the technology consequent upon it in the fields, for example, of medicine, law, historiography, are obvious. We are all the beneficiaries. One consequence, however, of this more empirically based approach to reality was that "the doctrine of creation, or a substitute for it, became in large measure the province of science, and scientists replaced theologians as the authorities for knowledge of the created world."[9] The results of the emergent new science and

---

7. Hayes, *Gift of Being*, 13.
8. Ward, *Pascal's Fire*, 25.
9. Gunton, "Doctrine of Creation," 151.

technology were very successful, and successful not just in terms of theory but in practical terms, making life increasingly easier and more comfortable for people.

At the same time, there emerged a downside to the new science. For many people the developing truths of science transitioned unconsciously into a blind faith in science known as "scientism." Scientism has been well described by the Irish philosopher Patrick Masterson as follows:

> I use the term "scientism" to describe the view that, insofar as the ultimate meaning and value of being in general and of human existence in particular can be reliably known, it is exclusively through reliance upon the method and achievements of empirical science and the exploitation of its remarkable technological possibilities. Scientism, in this sense, adopts empirical science as the key to understanding all aspects of human culture, which include its systems of representation, of standards, of expression, and of action.[10]

There can be no dismissal of either the importance of science (and technology) nor of its benefits. The problem is the exclusive reliance upon science and technology to yield the meaning and truth of the human condition and of all reality. Theology in this perspective becomes increasingly marginalized and religious faith is seen, and indeed too often seen, as a poor alternative to the demonstrable benefits of science.

Not only is theology in the strict sense of the word marginalized by scientism, but so also is a contemplative attitude to reality as a whole, a wondering attitude leading the one who wonders in the direction of praising gratitude. One contemporary commentator puts it like this: "Without contemplation, which is rooted in dispositions of receptive wonder, and without practical wisdom, which orders means to the ends of human flourishing, the human intellect can easily be reduced to its calculating and constructing

---

10. Masterson, *In Reasonable Hope*, 21. Masterson's book is a refreshing retrieval of classical realist metaphysics over against contemporary reductionist points of view.

capacities."[11] It does not have to be this way. Returning to the epigraph at the beginning of this chapter from Frances Young, "Science is as much as the genesis of wonder as a claim to comprehension." Yes, but the contemplative dimension of science, even one might say the *necessary* contemplative dimension of science, has been and is being pushed out by the pragmatic benefits of scientism.

The nineteenth century continued and indeed exacerbated the strained relationship between science and theology as theories of biological evolution began to posit the origins of the human species in earlier forms of life. Christians responded to these views of evolution in different ways. Some were open-minded and attempted to accommodate evolution within the fabric of the Christian tradition. Others, and perhaps the majority of nineteenth-century Christians, regarded evolution as inimical to Christian faith. These theories disturbed for many Christians the notion of God's unique creation of human beings. In 1859, Charles Darwin (1809–82) published his groundbreaking *On the Origin of the Species*. He postulated that the various species of plant and animal life have arisen through a gradual process of natural selection spanning eons and beginning with the simplest forms of life. The traditional Christian theology of creation was brought further into doubt. Reformed theologian Colin Gunton in summary form has this to say about the dominance of scientism: "God and the world were pictured in such a way that any continuing involvement became a kind of *tour de force*, and the well-known problem of the 'god of the gaps'—God's being driven progressively from the world—developed." Gunton is correct in this general description. Moreover, his historical-theological diagnosis of the situation is right on target: "Here is one place where the failure to maintain a trinitarian conception of the relation of God and the world through much of Christian history exacted a high price. The processes of criticism had driven out the old Platonic and Aristotelian way of conceiving the structure of the created world, but in their

---

11. Hibbs, *Theology of Creation*, 37. Hibbs's wide-ranging horizon in this book encompasses ecology, art and Pope Francis's encyclical *Laudato Si*, drawing upon the contributions of Jacques Maritain and contemporary artists and poets, but throughout the text, arguably, his pervasive concern is the loss of contemplative wonder.

place came a conception which excluded meaningful divine action altogether."[12]

God was pushed out further and further from an understanding of creation as a result of scientism. As this was taking place, philosophical approaches to God were also changing. The primary mode for naming God had been the vocative, addressing God as Thou—calling, invoking, beseeching, praising.[13] God became named less in the vocative as Thou, and more as a hypothetical Divine Subject to be examined. This Divine Subject, moreover, was becoming for many thinkers a "Supreme Being," and not immediately the Trinitarian-incarnational God of the Christian tradition, in whom one was enfolded through grace and to whom one related in worship, prayer and praise.[14]

Vatican Council I (1869–70) on Creation

General councils of the church are of central importance for Catholic Christians. Most Catholics understand that the First Vatican Council (1869–70) had to do with the infallibility of the church and of the papal office. Even as this was to the forefront of the Council's deliberations especially in the final months of its existence in 1870, there was more to the Council's concerns than that important issue, and one of these concerns had to do with the understanding of creation.

Responding to what were seen as serious challenges, both philosophical and theological, to the traditional understanding of creation, five carefully crafted canons set out the Council's understanding of creation.[15] They may be summarized in the following points. First, the whole world depends for its existence entirely on the activity of God the Creator. This point underscores that there

12. Gunton, "Doctrine of Creation," 152.
13. I am adapting here some sentiments from Soskice, *Naming God*, 34.
14. This displacing of God is well documented throughout Soskice's book, *Naming God*.
15. They may be found conveniently in Tanner, *Decrees of the Ecumenical Councils*, 809–10.

can be nothing "outside of God," as it were, that does not flow from God's creative power and activity alone. There can be no other source of reality than God. "There is no part of the reality of a creature which is independent of the Creator.... Without creation, there is absolutely nothing of anything existing."[16] Second, God is completely free in creating the world. Creation is a completely free act on God's part, not driven by any kind of compulsion or necessity. Third, the ultimate purpose of creation is to share in the goodness of God or, we might say, to give glory to God.

> The creature, in other words, glorifies God; it renders, consciously or unconsciously, glory to him as Creator. And the greater the extent to which the creature shares in the God-given goodness which is its creaturely existence, the more the creature exists for the greater glory of God: the more, then, does the creature correspond to the ultimate purpose of God's all creation.[17]

Theologian Robert Butterworth makes the solid point that, albeit unintentionally, this particular way of understanding creation, while it is utterly emphatic about the centrality of God's action in creating, "has nothing to do with Christ.... There must be root links between Christ and creation."[18] The root links between Christ and creation, so central to earlier Christian thinking, were to be rediscovered theologically in the twentieth century and continuing into the present day. We will look at some of the theologians who have made this rediscovery in the next chapter.

Creation, Evolution, and the Soul

Notwithstanding earlier debates about evolution from the nineteenth century onward, mainline Christian theology has embraced an evolutionary perspective. Two key issues were central to the debate: the seeming conflict with Scripture and the possible

---

16. Butterworth, *Theology of Creation*, 17.
17. Butterworth, *Theology of Creation*, 19.
18. Butterworth, *Theology of Creation*, 23.

implications of evolution theory for a theological understanding of the human person. "In regard to an apparent conflict with Scripture, the longstanding tension has been mitigated notably by two admissions. The first is the need to differentiate religious and scientific truth. The second is the imperative to advert to the literary forms used in the Bible."[19] For the most part Christian Scripture scholarship has come to terms with evolution theory, and something similar obtains in respect of Christian anthropology.

The problem here has been the conviction that while the human body may have developed from the evolutionary process, at least in the Catholic tradition the conviction was that the human soul was directly created by God. Pope Pius XII in his 1950 encyclical letter *Humani Generis* remarked, "For the Catholic faith obliges us to hold that souls are immediately created by God."[20] That particular statement "immediately created by God" is problematic. At best it may be understood as a way of expressing the special place of humankind in relation to God the Creator. However, the actual wording seems to suggest "the postulation of a recurrent 'intervention' by God each time a human being comes to be."[21] That meaning seems also to be present in the *Catechism of the Catholic Church*, par. 366: "The church teaches that every spiritual soul is created immediately by God—it is not produced by the parents—and also that it is immortal. It does not perish when it separates from the body at death, and it will be reunited with the body at the final resurrection."[22]

Among others, theologian Nicholas Lash (1934–2020) points out the strangeness of the thinking here.[23] He takes to task the soul-body dualism that appears to lie behind this way of thinking, as if the "soul" and the "body" were two distinct and quite separate entities, a dualism resisted in Aristotelian and Thomist thought, in which the soul is the form of the body. Lash asks two questions of

19. Carroll, *Towards a Story of the Earth*, 124.
20. Pope Pius XII, *Humani Generis*, par. 36.
21. Carroll, *Towards a Story of the Earth*, 128.
22. *Catechism of the Catholic Church*, par. 366.
23. Lash, "Are We Born and Do We Die?," 403–12.

this dualist viewpoint: Do human parents produce human beings? Do human beings die? The doctrine of the special creation of the individual soul immediately by God seems to require us to answer the first question in the negative because, according to this doctrine, parents only produce matter for the God-given soul to form. As to the second, many people seem to suppose that human beings do not die, only their bodies do. Arguing against this widespread but insufficiently reflective anthropological dualism and against the view that immortality is a natural property of human minds, Lash suggests that, whether we speak of "immortality" or of "resurrection," life from death is neither nature nor achievement but gift.

In a private communication from Professor Lash, lately Norris-Hulse Professor of Divinity, University of Cambridge of July 1, 2009, in response to a suggestion I made that parents "co-create" with God the human person, body and soul, this is what he said:

> For two reasons, I suspect that you are being a little too kind about the confusions expressed in what we might call the "official position." First, I don't think that the notion of "co-creation" gets us very far because, of course, in the sense that God creates, no creature does. Second, if the impulse were that of what you call "a laudable desire to recognize the creative action of God in *all* life" [Lash's stress], then, logically, we would have to say that the soul of every cabbage, caterpillar and cow is "created immediately by God." If I slightly rephrased the point you make, I think one could say that the notion of every human soul being created immediately by God is an attempt to express the sense of the preciousness and dignity of every individual human being. Unfortunately, I think that *also* at work is an almost Manichaean *under*estimation of the body.[24]

24. In this communication Lash continues as follows: "The authorities invoked in para. 366 of the Catechism are, I think, revealing. First, *Humani Generis*, where the reference, as I mention in the article, is hardly more than parenthetical. Second, Paul VI, *Credo of the People of God*, only says 'We believe in one only God, Father, Son and Holy Spirit, creator of things visible such as this world in which our transient life passes, of things invisible such as the pure spirits which are also called angels, and creator in each man of his spiritual and immortal soul'. Third, Lateran V, which, in the course of castigating various 16th-century 'neo-Aristotelean' errors, does not in fact mention the matter.

Creation in the Christian Tradition, Part 2

Pope Francis, *Laudato Si*

The year 2015 saw the publication of Pope Francis's encyclical letter *Laudato Si*. This was the same year in which Elizabeth Johnson's *Ask the Beasts* was published. The encyclical shows that the Pope was sensitive to and influenced by new currents of thought in the theology of creation, especially as regards ecology. The encyclical is lengthy and repays careful reading in its own right. This is how Irish systematic theologian Dermot Lane, who has made a thorough study of this document, helpfully summarizes something of the extremely positive responses this encyclical has evoked:

- A prophetic challenge for the twenty-first century.
- A game-changer;
- The most important encyclical in the life of the Catholic Church;
- A wake-up call for the world and the church;
- A moral milestone;
- A pastoral landmark;
- A revolutionary document.[25]

Lane goes on to describe the encyclical in his own words:

If anything, in warmly endorsing the Council of Vienne, it points in the other direction—'For the soul not only truly exists of itself and essentially as the form of the human body, as is said in the canon of our predecessor of happy memory, Pope Clement V, promulgated in the general council of Vienne, but it is also immortal; and further, for the enormous number of bodies into which it is infused individually, it can and ought to be and is multiplied.' I find it strange that this is the best that they could do!" I have quoted Nicholas Lash at some length because implicit in his position is a dismissal of the dualism that so often seems to present itself in church teaching, and that "immediately created by God" may be understood in a non-dualist but perfectly orthodox fashion, in accord with an evolutionary perspective. This is an area in Christian anthropology where much confusion continues to reign and much theological work needs to be done. Some promising lines may be found in Baglow, *Creation*, 61–76.

25. Lane, *Theology and Ecology in Dialogue*, 12.

> The encyclical addresses the ecological crisis from a variety of points of view: biblical, spiritual, theological, ethical, liturgical, economic and environmental. It is not in any sense a systematic treatment of the ecological crisis, but does draw on a variety of disciplines. It adopts the principle or methodology of "integral theology," which seeks to integrate the many insights of different disciplines into a coherent whole.[26]

Creation in the encyclical is fundamentally understood as gift.

Understanding creation in terms of "gift" is a common theme in the history of the tradition. Reflecting on the theology of creation, English systematic theologian Simon Oliver, using traditional theology and some contemporary philosophers, insists that for a gift to be truly gift, it must be received and acknowledged as such. He puts it in very ordinary and yet extraordinarily fine words. He offers the analogy of a child receiving a gift at Christmas. "The child has no economic power and is entirely dependent upon the daily gifts of her parents. At Christmas, the child's parents buy her a splendid present—a new bike. The child, however, has no means of buying her parents a gift; she has nothing that she has not already received. . . . [As she opens her gift] she turns to her parents, smiles and says, with joy and delight, 'thank you.'"[27] Understanding creation as gratuitous gift, an understanding consonant with the greater Christian tradition, brings us, we may say, to acclaim of our creating God, "How great Thou art!"

Conclusion

This all too brief "run through" some aspects of the theology of creation from the Renaissance to Pope Francis points up some conclusions. First, it is very difficult for many to move away from an almost exclusive anthropocentric understanding of creation to the more integral view of Pope Francis (and others). Many do not wish to relinquish the "comfort zone" afforded by this isolationist

---

26. Lane, *Nature Praising God*, 38.
27. Oliver, *Creation*, 147.

anthropocentrism. Second, the dualism in Christian thinking—"soul" and "body" as separate entities, for example—remains an impediment to accepting a more integrated approach to creation. One scholar, writing in 2003, commented: "Even until recently, creation seemed a poor relation within the theological family.... It is no exaggeration to say that 'creation theology' dragged out an anemic existence on the theological periphery."[28] If that was indeed the case, it is certainly not the situation of the theology of creation today. In the next chapter we shall see how some contemporary Christian thinkers are responding to these issues. Although the thinkers that will be considered approach the doctrine of creation from varying points of view, their theology is robustly Trinitarian and marked by what I have earlier described as the "creation-Christological nexus." Acknowledging the Triune God and the connection between Christ and creation demands more than an intellectual assent. As this chapter concludes, I want to return to some words of the Reformed theologian Colin Gunton that seem right on the mark. This is what he says: "We need to move away from seeing creation as a mere given to receiving it as gift to be cherished, perfected, and returned: as grace evoking gratitude. The heart of the matter is worship, for it is there that are presented and enacted both the Creator's redemptive interaction with his world and the response of the one in whom the creation becomes articulate."[29] Gunton seems to me absolutely correct. Creation is gift, and the Giver is God, and the heart of the matter is indeed worship in and through which we give thanks and praise. We are led to acclaim, "How great Thou art!"

---

28. Carroll, "An Essay in the Theology of Creation," 15.
29. Gunton, "The Doctrine of Creation," 155.

6

A Sprinkling of Contemporary Theologians on Creation

It is not a theologian's job to peddle scientific lore about the mode or process of creation.

Robert Butterworth[1]

Creation and incarnation are not two disparate and juxtaposed acts of God or two separate events of God; rather, creation and incarnation are two moments and two phases of the one process of God's self-giving and self-expression; the God who creates is the God who saves. In this respect, the whole creation, beginning with the Big Bang is incarnation.

Ilia Delio[2]

We need a number of models and images to represent divine action to ourselves, and each has its limitations as well as its possibilities.

Gabriel Daly[3]

1. Butterworth, *Theology of Creation*, 11.
2. Delio, *The Emergent Christ*, 153.
3. Daly, *Creation and Redemption*, 41.

A Sprinkling of Contemporary Theologians on Creation

Introduction

THE THREE OPENING CITATIONS from Butterworth, Delio, and Daly set the stage for an examination of the contributions of various theologians in this chapter. I take as standard for the traditional theology of creation the exceptionally fine book of Leo Scheffczyk (1920–2005), *Creation and Providence* (1970). This excellent book is part of the famed Herder "History of Dogma" and has been relied upon and quoted throughout this present work. After some forty pages dealing with scriptural approaches to creation and using contemporary exegesis, Scheffczyk proceeds through two hundred pages to engage the theology of creation principally through the lens of philosophy. It is a remarkable achievement. Half a century later (and indeed for some of our authors earlier than that) the theology of creation unfolds not only through Scripture and philosophy but also through conversation with contemporary science.

Common to all of the theologians that we shall consider is what we might call their theistic/metaphysical vision and their ecumenical openness. A theistic/metaphysical vision tells us how to speak of God. There is no neutral, no purely objective approach to understanding "God." Everyone pursuant of an understanding of God brings to that quest the story that she or he is. Quite simply, everyone *is* a story, or better, a story made up of countless other stories. Everyone brings to the theological task presuppositions that are emergent from familial, ecclesial, and cultural contexts. In other words, everyone is traditioned. We *see* God differently. That is not to say that there is no overlap between one person's seeing and another's, nor that all seeing of God is of equal value. That form of thoroughgoing relativism is nothing short of performative contradiction. What attracts to one form of seeing over against others, what is appealing about one system of metaphysics rather than another, is that it brings one's reflected experience to a depth of richness and vitality not matched by any alternative. It yields what the Scottish Presbyterian theologian, Allan D. Galloway, has called *sanitas* or wholeness, "the enjoyment of an integrity of response."[4] Or, changing the philosophical climate in the direction of Bernard Lonergan's brand of transcendental Thomism, a reflected metaphysical position, a reflected seeing of God and God's relations with created reality, is a *virtually unconditioned*, that is to say, no other alternative has the capacity satisfactorily to answer all relevant questions with suasive satisfaction.[5] A theistic system of thinking is very close to what the American Jesuit philosopher W. Norris Clarke calls "a personal psychological predisposition towards metaphysical thinking, something like a *metaphysical bent of mind*."[6] This predisposition toward metaphysical thinking, according to Clarke, is marked by two qualities: "a passion for unity, for seeing the universe and all things in it fit together as a whole, a longing for integration of thought and life based on the integration of reality itself," and "a sense of some kind of overall hidden harmony of the universe, which could be picked up and possibly spelled out if one listened carefully enough." Although arguably no metaphysics is ever complete, since completeness in any Christian interpretation is itself an eschatological condition, a "way of seeing" offers real and sustained nurture to one who wishes to see. By "ecumenical openness" I mean a movement out of a narrowly construed confessional approach to theology so that there is an enrichment from various Christian traditions, but also an openness to enlargement and enrichment from other perspectives, such as science and modern philosophy. Perhaps we may agree as Christians that "we do not want a divine dictator who would destroy our freedom; we want a heavenly Father who does not violate the universe and human freedom, a God who deals with us in love, not simply in power."[7] To this end I choose to focus on the contributions of six theologians: Pierre Teilhard de Chardin, John Macquarrie, John Polkinghorne, Roger Haight, Elizabeth Johnson, and Thomas Hosinski. Each one of them has his/her own distinctive way of reflecting on the theology of creation. At the same time, and

---

4. See Galloway, *Faith in a Changing Culture*, 51–63, especially 63.
5. See Lonergan, *Insight*, chapter 10, and *Method in Theology*, 57–99.
6. McCool, *Universe as Journey*, 50.
7. Baglow, *Creation*, 37.

informed not only by the tradition of Christian theology but also by science and contemporary philosophy, they seem to me to offer satisfying and persuasive approaches to the theology of creation.

Pierre Teilhard de Chardin, SJ (1881–1955)

There can be little doubt that the trailblazer for the application of evolutionary ideas to the theology of creation in the Catholic tradition was the French Jesuit Pierre Teilhard de Chardin. His hopeful perspectives and his non-adversarial stance *vis-à-vis* the world and particularly the world of science helped to pave the way for the new awakening that theologically was the "new theology" of the 1930s and 1940s and that ecclesially was to be Vatican II (1962–65).

Teilhard's spiritual and theological passion might be summarized in this fashion: "I would like to be able to have a great love for Christ in the *very act* of loving the universe. Is that a dream or a blasphemy? Besides union with God and union with the world, isn't there a union with God through the world?"[8] Teilhard recognized that for many educated people of his time—and, indeed, of our own time—Christianity seems too small, too insular, disconnected from contemporary, especially scientific experience. "The ecclesiastical directives and the preoccupations of the faithful are slowly sealing the Church in an artificial world of rituals, of routines, of pious practices, a world completely separated from the mainstream of life."[9] The French Jesuit priest-scientist wanted to counter this disconnect.

He read Henri Bergson's *Creative Evolution* in which "he found, or thought he found, a rationale for his new feeling of union with the vegetable and animal world. . . . For him 'Matter' and 'Spirit' were becoming two faces of the same coin."[10] Reading

---

8. Cited in Faricy, *Teilhard de Chardin's Theology*, 4.
9. Cited in Faricy, *Teilhard de Chardin's Theology*, 19.
10. Lukas and Lukas, *Teilhard*, 33–34.

Bergson helped to develop Teilhard's growing sense of the immanence of God in nature.

Two of his most famous works were composed in China where he was doing fieldwork as a paleontologist: in 1926–27 *The Divine Milieu*, a strongly experiential treatise on the spiritual life, and from 1938 to 1940 *The Phenomenon of Man*. Both of these important works fell foul of his Jesuit censors, not least due to his strongly evolutionist vision, the symbiosis of matter and spirit. He was prevented from publishing. In 1954, the year before he died he wrote to a friend: "Less and less do I see any difference now between research and adoration."[11] In a similar vein he wrote on Good Friday 1955 to a friend, "Evil is not 'catastrophic' (the fruit of some cosmic accident), but the inevitable side effect of the process of the cosmos unifying into God."[12]

A brief conspectus of some of his ideas will establish some of the reasons for his ever-growing popularity. Matter is all-important for Teilhard. "By means of all created things, without exception, the divine assails us, penetrates us, and moulds us."[13] This is no espousal of pantheism for Teilhard. It emerges, rather, from his profoundly Christocentric cosmology, two of his favorite New Testament passages being the Prologue to St. John's Gospel and Colossians 1:15–20. In both of these passages, as noted earlier in chapter 3, creation comes into being through the Word, and in the Johannine passage the Word becomes flesh. Matter, then, for Teilhard is never just matter, but is Trinitarian and Christocentric. It is the Divine Milieu. One commentator writes that "Teilhard is not far from Aquinas' notion that God is in all things by power, presence, and essence (ST 1a.8 ad.3), or . . . from the Eastern Fathers with their sense of the cosmos as the theater of divine energy."[14] Evolution for Teilhard has a direction toward higher degrees of material complexity, higher degrees of organization, and toward higher degrees of consciousness. In other words, the universe is

---

11. Lukas and Lukas, *Teilhard*, 328.
12. Lukas and Lukas, *Teilhard*, 342.
13. de Chardin, *The Divine Milieu*, 112.
14. Williams, "The Traditionalist," 114.

evolving toward greater spiritualization according to a law of what he called "complexity-consciousness." This is explicitly linked with Christian faith because as he understood it the universe is evolving toward a point/center that somehow is already present and that somehow is personal, and he identifies this personal center with Christ. Henri de Lubac describes his thoughts as follows: "The concrete Presence at the heart of the Universe, dominating it, animating it, and drawing it to him—the presence of a personal God—super-personal, i.e., ultra-personal—of a loving and provident God, of a God who can reveal himself, and has in fact revealed himself—of a God who is all Love—this was for Teilhard the supreme truth." At the same time, he was entirely opposed to the limitations of anthropomorphism: "To nine-tenths of those who see him from outside, the Christian God appears as a great landowner administering his estates."[15]

The Omega of reason, of Teilhard's physics of evolution, and of the Christ of revelation are one and the same reality. He grounds this way of thinking in the New Testament, especially in the cosmic-Christological affirmations of St. John and St. Paul. Thus, he combines the evolutionary concept of cosmogenesis with his Christian tradition so as to rethink cosmogenesis in terms of Christogenesis.

One of his most influential and popular books, written in 1927, "as prayerfully and uncontentiously as possible," was titled *The Divine Milieu*. The book was dedicated "to those who love the world" and espoused the notion that material reality was the necessary medium through which the human person reached God. The human spirit was not to be understood as an "insubstantial specter" but as the sum and essence of all the vitality and consistency of the body—as "Matter at its most incendiary stage."[16] In 1939, his Jesuit censors took him to task for "The Spiritual Phenomenon," the paper in which he challenged the Aristotelian distinction between spirit and matter. The paper implied that "germs of consciousness" necessarily existed in even the smallest particles

---

15. de Lubac, *Teilhard de Chardin*, 23–25.
16. de Lubac, *Teilhard de Chardin*, 104.

of matter. This viewpoint was to make its way into the most systematic articulation of his vision, *The Phenomenon of Man* (1959).

John Macquarrie (1919–2007)

John Macquarrie was one of the most influential Anglican theologians of the twentieth century.[17] Traditional Christian theology taught, as we have seen, that the world was made out of nothing, *creatio ex nihilo*, by the agency of God. This way of thinking entailed that creation came about without any preexisting matter, as an entirely free act on God's part. Having come into being and being sustained in being by God, creation was also thought of as moving toward its end/*telos* in God's purpose. "The divine act of origination is thus inseparable from God's continuing providential activity, preserving and governing that which has been made."[18] Developments in both philosophy and science since the Enlightenment have called the classical understanding of creation into question in various ways, so contemporary theology attempts to restate in a corrective fashion some elements of that doctrine.

At this point, it will be helpful to note briefly just how problematic it is to flesh out the relation between God and creation, using the words of Allan Douglas Galloway, Macquarrie's fellow-student in Glasgow's Faculty of Divinity, as they both prepared for Presbyterian ministry in the Church of Scotland.

> [Macquarrie] is here exploring a new way of tackling an ancient problem for which no wholly satisfactory and consistent solution has ever been offered—that of God's relation to his creation. If we remove God in impassive sovereignty beyond all interior relation to the world we end with a deistic being very unlike the living God of the Bible. If we bring God unequivocally within the *present* world we end with a pagan divinity. If we think of the

---

17. See Cummings, *John Macquarrie*, and in much greater detail *The Theology of John Macquarrie (1919–2007)*.

18. Webster, "Creation," 95.

present world as unequivocally in God, then we deny the independence, contingency and freedom of creation.[19]

There being no "wholly satisfactory and consistent solution" to describing the relation between God and creation, it makes sense to offer various models of creation as one way to move toward a satisfactory approach to the question that is both Christian and reasonable, and that is how Macquarrie proceeds.

For John Macquarrie, "The question is not, How did the world begin? or, Who made it? but rather What does it mean to be a creature? or, How does it affect our understanding of ourselves and our world to believe that we and it are creations of God?"[20] Starting from the basic fact of human existence and the questions to which that gives rise does not mean that there is a supremacy to human beings that makes them lords over creation. Rather, the human position *vis-à-vis* creation is that of stewards. Traditionally Christian theology has spoken of *creatio ex nihilo/creation out of nothing*. Macquarrie's understanding of this is that "it draws attention to the fact that any particular being stands, so to speak between nothing and Being. It *is*, in so far as it participates in Being, but at any time it may cease to be."[21] To be is a gift from Being-letting-be, from God, and evokes a sense of dependence. "Being lets-be, but it does so only at risk to itself, only by giving itself and going out into openness. To see this is to see that the creativity of Being or God is basically the same as the love of God."[22] This leads Macquarrie to posit the analogy of the artist and her or his work. The artist puts something of herself into her artistic creation and in an analogous way the Creator God may be seen as not only transcendent, the source and origin of all that is, but also as immanent, present-and-manifest throughout all of creation.

---

19. Galloway is speaking here of Wolfhart Pannenberg's theology. Changing the reference to Macquarrie as I have done nonetheless gives a very clear sense of the ongoing problematic between God and creation. See Galloway, *Wolfhart Pannenberg*, 96–97.
20. Macquarrie, *Principles of Christian Theology*, 212.
21. Macquarrie, *Principles of Christian Theology*, 215.
22. Macquarrie, *Principles of Christian Theology*, 217.

If we were to look upon the whole sweep of the Christian tradition in respect of the doctrine of creation, according to Macquarrie, two fundamental models present themselves. The first model is that of "making," the understanding of creation found especially in the Scriptures. In his judgment this model stresses the transcendence of God, emphasizing the difference between God and his creation. The second model is that of emanation, that creation proceeds out from God, and certainly finds its roots in the Neoplatonic elements of the patristic authors. This model stresses the immanence of God, pointing up God's affinity with and closeness to his creation. Both models are necessary, in Macquarrie's opinion, in order to do justice to the Mystery of God, who is both transcendent and immanent, each model correcting the other. "It is all a question of maintaining a right balance of transcendence and immanence, and perhaps this is best done by holding side by side in their tension with one another the models of making and emanation."[23] This both-and approach is typical of Macquarrie's dialectical methodology.

In his 1967 book *God and Secularity* Macquarrie states that there are five specific Christian doctrines that are of first importance in opening up the total Christian vision, and the first of these is the doctrine of creation. Based on the affirmation of Genesis 1:31 that "God saw everything that he had made, and behold, it was very good" this Christian doctrine distances itself from any perspective that would view the material world "as somehow inherently evil."[24] God is the prior condition of the existence of anything. "The world does not exist of itself, and it is not an ultimate. To understand its significance, we have to see it in its relation to God, who has brought it into being."[25] A major consequence of this perspective is that humankind are corporately the guardians or stewards of creation, not its masters or owners.

Taking what Macquarrie calls a minimal sense of God as "a reality that is intelligent and purposeful" then it is possible to see

23. Macquarrie, *Principles of Christian Theology*, 219.
24. Macquarrie, *God and Secularity*, 132.
25. Macquarrie, *God and Secularity*, 132.

in the universe certain features that point to "God." "The universe seems to be a highly orderly affair, built up of a limited number of basic types of particles which have the capacity for combining in innumerable complex patterns. Furthermore, it is a universe that has itself brought forth beings having intelligence and purpose."[26] At the same time, there is randomness and ambiguity so that these observations do not constitute a knock-down proof of the existence of the Creator, "but we can say at least that the claim that God (understood still in a fairly minimal way) is the author of the world is not an absurd idea."[27]

If we then move on from the minimal view of God to the understanding of God as Creator in the Judeo-Christian tradition, we can go further, and we are enabled to do so by considering the analogy of the artist and his or her work. An artist we may say "creates" and does not merely "make." When an artist creates a painting, he puts something of himself into that painting so that we may say that the picture is "an extension of the artist himself. He is now in the picture, just as the picture had been in him."[28] We now have a sense of the Artist-God's presence in creation, but Macquarrie presses on to maintain that the creation was also "a self-emptying."

> So when we begin to analyze the idea of creation, we find that it is not so much an exercise of power as rather an exercise of love and generosity, an act of self-limitation and even of self-humiliation on the part of God. His love and generosity lead him to share existence with his creatures.... Although we say that God did this "in the beginning," that is only our mythological way of saying what we believe to be God's nature from eternity. He has always been creative love, and it is love rather than power that is his primary attribute.[29]

---

26. Macquarrie, *The Humility of God*, 3.
27. Macquarrie, *Humility of God*, 3.
28. Macquarrie is fond of the analogy of the artist and his work for God and creation, and here the reference is to his *The Humility of God*, 4.
29. Macquarrie, *Humility of God*, 4–5.

At this point, Macquarrie is very close to the meaning of the axiom *Bonum est diffusivum sui/Goodness is diffusive of itself*, generally attributed to Pseudo-Dionysius but with roots in other patristic authors and present in St. Thomas Aquinas. If we take "love" as a synonym for "goodness," then creation exists because God as Love desires to share existence, since "Goodness itself is inherently fecund."[30] This leads Macquarrie to affirm: "The God who creates is not just some vague Supreme Intelligence or anything of the sort. He is the God who is always coming out from himself in love and sharing and self-giving, and the commitment that he makes to his creation already points forward to the fuller involvement of the incarnation and the passion."[31] This is a prominent theme in Macquarrie. Earlier in 1967 in his *God and Secularity* he wrote: "It is as if the incarnation focuses in a single point what God has, in a sense, been doing always and everywhere; and if, in an ambiguous world, God's presence and action are often hidden, the Christian claim is that he is signally present and manifest in Jesus Christ, the incarnate Word, so that Christ becomes the center for the interpretation of the whole."[32] The doctrines of creation and incarnation go together. "God, we may say, is so intimately involved with his creation that in a remarkable way Creator and creature become one in incarnation. But this can only be because the possibility (we might even be permitted to say, the purpose) is already there in creation, and in the transcendent-immanent relation between expressive Being and the beings."[33] Macquarrie's way of thinking leads to a theophanous sense of creation, something that has been a constant in Christian theology. Behind the sensible presentation of creation in all its wonderful expressions lies the ever-generous and self-giving Giver that is God. Arguably,

---

30. The phrase comes from the Eriugena scholar John F. Gavin, in *A Celtic Christology*. Bernhard-Thomas Blankenhorn, OP, treats of this notion in Aquinas, but judges that while it leads to the relationality of all creation (and Macquarrie would agree), it does not lead to the relationality of God's own being. See Blankenhorn, "The Good as Self-Diffusive in Thomas Aquinas," 803–37.

31. Macquarrie, *Humility of God*, 5.

32. Macquarrie, *God and Secularity*, 133.

33. Macquarrie, *Principles of Christian Theology*, 220–21.

since at least the Enlightenment and the scientific exploration and quantification of reality, there has taken place an increasing reduction in this traditional theophanous sense. Macquarrie's *oeuvre* may be seen as a project for its recovery and retrieval.

John Polkinghorne (1930–2021)

John Polkinghorne was an Anglican priest and theologian, but prior to that he had a distinguished career as a physicist, and so he is well placed to speak of creation from the perspectives of both theology and science. As he thinks of creation, both theologically and scientifically, his point of departure is the doctrine of the Trinity. "A deeply intellectually satisfying candidate for the title of a true 'Theory of Everything' is in fact provided by Trinitarian theology."[34] Polkinghorne teases out this grammar of the doctrine of the Trinity so as to encompass creation:

> Pursuing that point [God's divine power in creating] surely involves appeal to the divine love that has willed the existence of the truly other so that, through creation, this love is also bestowed outside the perichoretic exchange between the Persons of the Holy Trinity. Creation exists because God gives to it a life and a value of its own.[35]

Further teasing out this way of thinking, Polkinghorne suggests seven "scientifically disclosed features of our universe" consonant, and more than consonant, with the Triune God.

1. *A deeply intelligible universe.* The universe has proved to be "astonishingly rationally transparent, and the human mind remarkable apt to the comprehension of its structure." In other words, the universe/creation does not seem to be just a happy accident. More than that, Polkinghorne goes on to say: "Whether acknowledged or not, it is the Holy Spirit,

---

34. Polkinghorne, *Science and the Trinity*, 61. The following citations from Polkinghorne are taken from pages 60–86.

35. Polkinghorne, "Kenotic Creation and Divine Action."

the Spirit of truth (John 15.26), who is at work in the truth-seeking community of scientists. That community's repeated experiences of wonder at the disclosed order of the universe are, in fact, tacit acts of worship of its Creator" (p. 65).

2. *A universe with a fruitful history.* The universe originated in the event known as the Big Bang, some fourteen billion years ago, and evolved into complex structures. "After 14 billion years of evolving history, that same universe has become richly diverse and structured, with ourselves the most complex consequences of which we are aware. . . . It is a striking fact that that initial ball of energy has become the home of saints and mathematicians. . . . Might there be some purpose behind it all?" (p. 66). While there was no life for fourteen billion years, Polkinghorne makes the comment: "There is a real sense in which the universe was pregnant with the possibility of carbon-based life almost from the moment of the Big Bang onwards. Its physical fabric was then the exact form necessary to allow the eventual emergence of life" (p. 68). His perspective suggests that the universe knew we were coming.

3. *A relational universe.* "It has turned out that even the subatomic world cannot be treated atomistically! Twentieth-century science has revealed a deep-seated interconnectivity present in the fabric of the physical world" (p. 74). As Polkinghorne has it: "We may need to contemplate the possibility that persons participate in some greater solidarity than atomized Western society is able to recognize" (p. 73). Human beings are relational, just as all creation is relational, reflecting the Divine Relationality that is the Triune God. Reality is relational: one atom is no atom; one person is no person; one Divine Person is no Divine Person.

4. *A universe of veiled reality.* Despite the rational transparency, "quantum theory has shown us that it is cloudy and fitful at its subatomic roots. . . . If that epistemic specificity is true of subatomic physics, it is surely even more important to

recognize a similar truth in relation to the knowledge of God" (pp. 76–77).

5. *A universe of open process.* "The scientific picture implies that creation is a world of true becoming and not a world of static being.... Here order and openness so interlace that the state of affairs is neither so rigid that nothing really new can ever come about, nor so haphazard that nothing new can ever persist.... A Trinitarian theology of nature has some resonance with this insight. The Father is the fundamental ground of creation's being, while the Word is the source of creation's deep order and the Spirit is ceaselessly at work within the contingencies of open history. The fertile interplay of order and openness. Operating at the edge of chaos, can be seen to reflect the activities of Word and Spirit, the two divine Persons that Irenaeus called 'the hands of God.'" (pp. 80–81). This understanding of Polkinghorne's is especially important. It is firmly grounded in the doctrine of the Trinity, an important emphasis for him. As he develops his Trinitarian awareness, he is attempting to show the presence of the Trinity to creation with the eternal Word as the source of the order in creation and the Holy Spirit as the ceaseless energy leading us into the future. God is not remote from creation but deeply invested in creation.

6. *An information-generating universe.* On the threshold of new developments in scientific understanding, not least due to computer technology. The information seems more and more to suggest a dynamic *pattern*. Polkinghorne relates this to the doctrine of providence. God is a hidden God, but acting and guiding creation and history. This conviction follows from his deep grounding in the Trinity. If God is not remote but deeply and permanently present to his creation, then Providence must be seen as a consequence of this conviction. God may be hidden, that is to say not empirically demonstrable, but God's presence to creation opens us up to confidence, trust, and gratitude.

7. *A universe of eventual futility.* In response to the question "What is the future of creation, of our world?" there appear to be, from a scientific point of view, two possibilities: the explosive force of the initial Big Bang, driving matter apart, and the contractive force of gravity, pulling matter together. As Polkinghorne reads contemporary cosmologists they seem to favor that expansion will predominate and the regular reports of discoveries in space/cosmology are continuous reminders of this expansion. At the same time he writes, "Either way the cosmos is condemned to eventual futility. It is as certain as can be that carbon-based life will everywhere prove to have been a transient episode in its history" (p. 85). This is difficult to absorb for the ordinary Christian. What does "eventual futility" mean for the person of Christian faith? Polkinghorne continues confidently in this vein: "Personally, I do not think that the knowledge of the universe's death on a timescale of very many tens of millions of years raises any greater theological difficulties than does the even more certain knowledge of our own deaths on timescales of tens of years. If there is hope, either for the universe or for us, it can only lie in the eternal faithfulness of God. . . . Also important, I believe, is the witness of the empty tomb, for the fact that the Lord's glorified body is the transmuted form of his dead body speaks to me that in Christ there is a destiny not for humanity only, but also for matter, and so for creation as a whole" (p. 86). This is well put. Trust and confidence in the future, for ourselves and for creation, lies in the faithfulness of God expressed *par excellence* we may say in the resurrection of our Lord Jesus Christ. The resurrection confirms our hope and confidence both for ourselves and for all creation. This for me is the very heart of Polkinghorne's understanding. While it is not in any sense really possible for us to grasp the final and definitive form of creation from science, it seems to me that native human hope and traditional Christian belief about the incarnation and resurrection of Jesus both challenge us, indeed invite us, to remain open "to the mystery that the created universe

is and can yet become."[36] For Christians, as it was also for John Polkinghorne, this remaining open is strengthened and supported and confirmed by ongoing worship, prayer, and ever deeper encounter with our Lord Jesus Christ.

Roger Haight, SJ (born 1936)

Roger Haight is a well-known Catholic theologian, perhaps especially for his work on Christology.[37] More recently he has turned his attention to the relationships between science and the theology of creation in his *Faith and Evolution*.[38] This volume is full of insights that spark a renewed interest in the theology of creation.

Haight begins with "Theological Concepts of God," foundational for any understanding of God and creation, and he outlines five traditional but contemporary approaches: God as pure act and being is the first approach. This is the perspective of St. Thomas Aquinas who proposed the understanding of God as "Being itself, of itself subsistent." Most students of theology will readily recognize this language since it has permeated much of the Christian tradition. "All beings have a being that is limited by the kind of being it is and the individuality that instantiates it. By contrast, the essence or nature or kind of being that is God is itself the pure action of being and is not limited. God is subsistent being, being without any limitation and thus infinite" (p. 64). God's very nature is "to be."

Closely related to this is the second concept of God, God as "Ground of Being." This language for God is associated with Paul Tillich, but Haight points out that it is also to be found in the medieval Dominican mystic Meister Eckhart (ca. 1260–ca. 1328). If God is the Ground of Being, then God may be expected to manifest himself to humankind in what Tillich calls "ecstatic reason."

---

36. This is the language of Hayes, *Gift of Being*, 123.

37. Haight, *Jesus, Symbol of God*.

38. Haight, *Faith and Evolution*. The following page references will be to this text.

"Human reason possesses an extraordinary ability to transcend the constraints of an ordinary situation, and 'the mind is grasped by mystery, namely, by the ground of being and meaning'" (p. 63). Tillich's God, as the Ground of Being, must be transcendent, similar to Aquinas, and again like Aquinas, God must also be immanent, "all things are rooted in God's power of being that sustains things from within" (p. 65). God is neither remote from his creation, nor is he to be thought of simplistically as the sum total of all this is. God is both the source of every being and the depth of every being.

Haight's third theological concept is derived from Mennonite theologian Gordon Kaufman (1925–2011), "God as serendipitous creativity."[39] Thinking less of God as the cause of reality and more as the dynamic energy of reality, God is understood as the mystery of creativity. "Kaufman is not moving from God to an idea of creator God; he is moving from an idea of creativity and trying it out as a metaphor for God" (p. 66). While this might immediately seem strange as an approach to God, it is founded in the human experience of creativity, the capacity to create oneself anew in however limited a way, and also new ways of engaging scientific discoveries. The energy that drives creativity is God. Haight writes:

> This definition of what God is has the advantage of drawing into itself the awesome conceptions of reality that science has most recently provided our imaginations. These are actually statistical notions that blow open and leave our minds gaping. And behind all the groping for adequate images for the age, size, energy, and intricate dynamism of reality, we may be able to accept a mystery that goes by the name of serendipitous creativity. (p. 67)

Fourth is God as incomprehensible mystery. This language is closely associated with the theology of Karl Rahner, SJ (1904–84). With roots in Aquinas, Kant and Hegel, and existentialism, God is approached as the mystery within which every human participates in virtue of existing. That gives expression to the immanence of God. It also points to God's transcendence as the human person, as "spirit in the world" grounded within God's immanent presence, is

---

39. See Kaufman, *In Face of Mystery*.

also inevitably (but not necessarily consciously) moving toward a final horizon that may be understood as God as transcendent. In Haight's words:

> Incomprehensible mystery carries a pervasive and comprehensive character that can accompany human existence in life across time. The metaphor of a horizon helps to describe this. God's relation to the world is not as a being relating to other beings, but as the grounding power of being: "The infinite expanse which can and does encompass everything cannot itself be encompassed." This presence of God to the world as ground describes a permanent horizon of existence and not merely a subjective experience. And the consciousness of it can run very deep. (p. 68)

Finally, there is God as transcendent presence. This way of thinking derives, according to Haight, from the contemporary theologian Thomas O'Meara, and absorbs some aspects of the other theological conceptions of God into itself.

> It does not compete with the other conceptions but provides a distinctive focusing image that reflects human experience.... A real transcendent Presence makes itself known within human experience. It appeals to a common experience of believers in God that some mysterious power works within and is irreducible to anything that is caused either by themselves or their environment. Many people have experiences of transcendence; such experience seems common enough to consider it a universal possibility. (p. 68)

These five theological principles, of course, are far more complex than this very summary account yields, but they do provide Haight with a firm and secure footing in contemporary theology from which to consider his theology of creation.

"The age and size of the universe seem to dwarf the human and dethrone anthropocentrism; the right integrity of nature seems to edge out God's intervention in the world and our lives; the randomness of evolution seems to subvert confidence in divine purpose; scientists do not speak of God and do not need the divine."[40] There is an element of hyperbole, I believe, in this description. Nonetheless, in its own way it points to the problematic that Christian believers and theologians experience in talking about God in relation to creation today. Leaving aside what Haight calls "baby language" for God and God's relation to the world, Haight posits three points. The first point is that the essence of creation in a Christian context "consists of an ontological relationship that is not empirically perceptible but that can be experienced in a rudimentary way."[41] This opens up various lines of thought. For example, it clearly distinguishes the scientific approach to creation which asks the question, "How did creation come about? How did it evolve?" from the more existential and fundamentally Christian question, "Why is creation there at all? Why am I?"

The second point is that divine transcendence and divine immanence include each other. "God is not *a* being that is infinite, but, like a verb, God is act or energy or dynamism. Once we construe God as not *a* being and not related externally to finite beings as objects to objects, transcendence and immanence can begin to coalesce into a unified or nondual reciprocity."[42] St. Thomas Aquinas and the others mentioned in the five theological principles concerning God would undoubtedly endorse what Haight is proposing here. Because God is not a thing, not an entity, even the supreme entity among other entities, God is transcendent. Because God in Christian theology (and, indeed, in the other Abrahamic traditions of thinking) is understood to be the source of everything that is, God is immanent.

At the same time, Haight insists that "the creating act of God is unimaginable and impenetrable mystery. God's action shares in the definition of God as incomprehensible mystery. We talk about God creating, but we literally know nothing about it in any positive sense."[43]

40. Haight, *Faith and Evolution*, 70.
41. Haight, *Faith and Evolution*, 70.
42. Haight, *Faith and Evolution*, 72.
43. Haight, *Faith and Evolution*, 73.

A consequence of Haight's way of thinking has to do with God and time. God, as transcendent, is outside time and so

> God's purpose for the world and its execution does not consist of temporal unfolding. God remains creating Presence to all that is, and all that becomes, all that was and will be, already is present to God. This framework of absolute mystery and Presence renders the very idea of a divine intervention in the world mistaken, an anthropomorphic confusion. It imagines that God accomplishes things one after the other.[44]

It is obvious that Haight has moved away from certain aspects of what have taken to be classical theism, still much present in catechesis and preaching. He is calling for the abandonment of an infantile approach to God and creation and for the adoption of a more reflective, experiential, mature and adult approach to these complex issues of Christian faith. That does not lead him, however, to what might be thought of as a deistic perspective, a perspective that lacks the central concerns of personal devotion. Haight writes:

> Another fundamental moral disposition that follows an understanding of creation is gratitude. The Christian spontaneously thinks of God creating freely and believes that love drives the enterprise. When this understanding of all reality has its scope narrowed to the single person's existence, the natural response is gratitude. When one achieves a certain amount of self-possession, sheer appreciation of and gratefulness for one's being seem to be an appropriate part of one's identity. Gratitude to help define the freedom or moral disposition of the Christian.[45]

Haight has taken us for the lofty heights of abstract theological thought to the threshold of worship and personal prayer.

---

44. Haight, *Faith and Evolution*, 77.
45. Haight, *Faith and Evolution*, 81.

How Great Thou Art

Elizabeth A. Johnson (born 1941)

Elizabeth Johnson, a religious of the Sisters of St. Joseph of Brentwood, New York, has had a distinguished career as a systematic theologian, ending her professional career at Fordham University, New York. In recent years she has turned her attention to the theology of creation, particularly in two books. In her 2015 book *Ask the Beasts: Darwin and the God of Love* she engages science with the Christian tradition in a very fruitful way, yielding new insights into the theology of creation.[46] Developing these ideas three years later but drawing them into dialogue with the Cross of Christ, Johnson published *Creation and the Cross*.[47]

In *Ask the Beasts* Johnson gives emphasis to the central issue of all creation praising God. This is what she says: "By virtue of being created, of being held in existence by the loving power of the Creator Spirit, all beings give glory to God simply by being themselves."[48] Here she joins not only the psalmist in acknowledging creation's praise of the Creator, but also the understanding of St. Thomas Aquinas as he emphasizes in his theology of creation that God holds everything in being.

Creation and the Cross is interesting not least because it is structured as a dialogue between Elizabeth and Clara as they search out various aspects of the theology of creation. My interest is especially in what Johnson calls "deep incarnation," a phrase coined by the Danish theologian Niels Gregersen. Johnson writes, including citing Gregersen's work:

> [The phrase] is starting to be used in theology to indicate the radical divine reach in Christ through human flesh all the way down into the living web of organic life with its growth and decay, amid the wide processes of evolving nature that beget and sustain life. As he writes, "In Christ, God enters into the biological tissue of creation in order to share the fate of biological existence. . . . In

---

46. Johnson, *Ask the Beasts*.
47. Johnson, *Creation and the Cross*.
48. Johnson, *Ask the Beasts*, 276.

> the incarnate One, God shares the life conditions of foxes and sparrows, grass and trees, soil and moisture." The saving God became a human being, who was part of the wider human community, which shares the membrane of life with other creatures, all made from cosmic material, and vulnerable to death and disintegration.[49]

This is the traditional Christological doctrine of the incarnation but in a new dress. The new dress is the emphasis, provided by developments in biological science, of the integration of all creation in the web of organic life. Johnson continues:

> Think of it this way. As a creature of earth, Jesus was a complex living unit of minerals and fluids, an item in the carbon, oxygen, and nitrogen cycles. The atoms comprising his body were once part of other creatures. The genetic structure of the cells in his body were kin to flowers, fish, frogs, finches, foxes, the whole community of life that descended from common ancestors in the ancient seas.[50]

This way of describing the incarnation of the Lord Jesus fleshes out just what incarnation, deep incarnation, means. In the incarnation God has wedded himself integrally to his creation, with all that entails. Through the death of Jesus on the cross God enters fully into the darkness of death, death that marks every form of organic life. This is what Gregersen refers to as the *tenebrae creationis*, the

---

49. Johnson, *Creation and the Cross*, 184–85. Further brief helpful comment on "deep incarnation" may be found in Lane, *Nature Praising God*, 79–81, and more fully in Edwards, *Deep Incarnation*. A central paragraph from Niels Gregersen shared by Edwards (p. 21) is worth reading: "'Deep Incarnation' is the view that God's own Logos (Wisdom and Word) was made flesh in Jesus the Christ in such a comprehensive manner that God, by assuming the particular life story of Jesus the Jew from Nazareth, also conjoined the material conditions of creaturely existence ('all flesh'), shared and ennobled the fate of all biological life forms ('grass' and 'lilies'), and experienced the pain of sensitive creatures ('sparrows' and 'foxes') from within. Deep incarnation thus presupposes a radical embodiment that reaches into the roots (*radices*) of material and biological existence as well as into the darker sides of creation: the *tenebrae creationis*."

50. Johnson, *Creation and the Cross*, 185–86.

"darkness of creation." Again citing Gregersen, Johnson continues: "Understood in this way the death of Christ becomes an icon of God's redemptive co-suffering with all sentient life as well as the victim of social competition."[51] The death of organic entities leads from them to new forms of life. New life emerges from death. As some would have it nature itself, creation itself, bears the stamp of the cross and may be described as cruciform.[52]

Good Friday's death of Jesus on the cross was not the last word. Easter Day follows with the resurrection of Jesus. This leads Johnson onward to consider the meaning of the resurrection not only for the Lord Jesus but for all creation. This is what she writes:

> Recall that what resurrection means in the concrete is not seriously imaginable to us who still live within the time-space grid of our known universe. Yet the empty tomb stands as an historical marker for the God of creation who can act with a power that transfigures biological existence itself. The Easter narratives witness that the crucified Jesus did not die into nothingness but into the embrace of the ineffable God who gives life, the first fruits of all the human dead. His destiny means that our hope does not merely clench at a possibility, but stands on the irrevocable ground of what has already transpired in him. . . . As the first fruit of an abundant harvest, the risen Jesus Christ pledges the future for all the dead, not only the dead of the human species but of all species. In Jesus crucified and risen, God who graciously gives life

---

51. Johnson, *Creation and the Cross*, 188.

52. The philosopher Holmes Rolston III is one of the scholars who talks about the cruciform nature of creation. See his remarkable essay "Kenosis and Nature," in which we find this representative sentiment on page 60: "Every organism is plunged into a struggle in which goodness is given only as it is fought for. Every life is chastened and christened, straitened and baptized in struggle. Everywhere there is vicarious suffering. The global earth is a land of promise, and yet one that has to be died for. The story is a passion play long before it reaches the Christ. Since the beginning, the myriad creatures have been giving up their lives as a ransom for many. In that sense, Jesus is not the exception to the natural order, but a chief exemplification of it."

to the dead and brings into being the things that do not exist will redeem the whole cosmos.[53]

It is not easy to understand what resurrection means for humankind, let alone what it means for all sentient beings. Johnson helpfully comments:

> Stay aware of the danger of literalizing, or reducing "heaven" to life on earth as we know it, only on a grander scale. The transformation to come escapes our imagination. It is true to say, though, that deep resurrection encourages us to include every creature of flesh in the hoped-for future. Each will be blessed according to its own nature as part of the whole creation that will be made new.[54]

This is certainly helpful and takes us as far as it is possible to go in creative reflection on the matter. At the very least, Johnson's perspective releases us from a too anthropocentric view of creation and resurrection.

Thomas E. Hosinski, CSC (1946–2022)

Thomas Hosinski was a Holy Cross priest who taught theology at the University of Portland. One of his major interests was in the conversation between Christian theology and process thought. Process thought is complex but, among other things, it may be understood as a way to escape from certain philosophical premises of Greek philosophy that have exercised enormous influence in the Christian tradition. "The God of the Process philosophers is conceived of as a dialectical correction to the cosmic tyrant who stands apart from, and remains unaffected by, the world he has created."[55] That, I believe, would be a fair albeit partial assessment

---

53. Johnson, *Creation and the Cross*, 190.
54. Johnson, *Creation and the Cross*, 192.
55. Daly, *Creation and Redemption*, 15. However, it is to be noted that Daly goes on to point out that "it would be incorrect to suppose that Process theology and philosophy are uniform in their approach. Process thinkers share certain preoccupations, but they can differ from one another both in terminology

of process thought for Hosinski, the title of whose University of Chicago Divinity School doctoral dissertation is "Process, Insight and Empirical Method: An Argument for the Compatibility of the Philosophies of Alfred North Whitehead and Bernard J. F. Lonergan." His final book before his premature death was *The Image of the Unseen God* (2017). It is to this publication that we turn our attention for his insights into the theology of creation.

> So often the way people talk about creation makes it seem like a magical act, that God simply wilted and, poof, the universe comes into being. We must have great humility here, but we ought to be able to suggest some way of understanding how God creates that squares with our experience and with what we know of the universe through science.[56]

In the broad process approach to God's creation, creation is not only far from being some kind of afterthought for God, who is so to speak complete in himself, but rather it is the very nature of God to be Creator.[57]

Hosinski asks the question, "If God is the Creator in the sense of being the ultimate ground of order and the ultimate source of potentiality that makes the universe possible, how is God directly involved in the creation of each agent in the universe?"[58] This is how Hosinski answers the question:

> In each moment we inherit the energy of our existence from the physical processes of the universe, but ultimately from God. At each moment God creates us by endowing us with all the possibilities open to us in the situation we face, with the drive to make something of ourselves at that moment (in other words, the drive to

---

and in points of emphasis. . . . Perhaps the best expedient is to see Process theology less as a finished position than as a needed corrective to certain elements in traditional theism" (pp. 20–22).

56. Hosinski, *The Image of the Unseen God*, 110.
57. See Daly, *Creation and Redemption*, 22.
58. Hosinski, *Image of the Unseen God*, 113–14.

actualize one of the possibilities), and with freedom, our share in the divine life.[59]

In his understanding, God is attracting us as present in each of us toward making actual the best possibility. Thus understood, "God creates us not by determining us but by *empowering* us, by giving us what we need to create ourselves."[60] God respects human freedom but, following Whitehead, Hosinski goes on to insist on freedom as an aspect of every created agent. Freedom is not unique to humans. Working from our own experience of freedom and equally as part of and in continuity with the whole of nature, freedom is extended to every entity. This does not mean, of course, that freedom is the same for every created agent. Alfred North Whitehead (1861–1947), with whom Hosinski is in agreement, "argues that all agents in the universe have some degree of freedom, even if it is so minimal that we cannot ordinarily recognize it. If we are unwilling to extend freedom this pervasively to all the agents of the universe, then we are faced with the very difficult problem of explaining how freedom can suddenly arise in a universe without it."[61] This does not mean, however, that all agents are conscious. Just that they have some degree of freedom. "Consciousness is restricted to animals; but experience, the power to feel, select, and actualize possibilities, and some degree of freedom are present in all agents, conscious or not, down to quantum events."[62] This idea can be challenging, but if we find it to be so, perhaps that may have to do with a too human-centered view of creation that is discontinuous with creation as such. The more science probes into the whole of creation the more does it demonstrate continuities between all levels of reality.

Whitehead did not believe that freedom understood as creativity was a gift from God. Differing from Whitehead on this point, Hosinski insists that the freedom that all agents have

---

59. Hosinski, *Image of the Unseen God*, 114.
60. Hosinski, *Image of the Unseen God*, 115.
61. Hosinski, *Image of the Unseen God*, 115.
62. Hosinski, *Image of the Unseen God*, 115.

in some degree is a gift, "the power of God's own life graciously shared with the creatures of the universe, not a force independent of God," as suggested by Whitehead.[63] From physics we know that the universe is fundamentally energy, energy that can take on many forms, including becoming matter, and evolving on from matter into ever more complex forms. Hosinski goes on to illustrate this process by drawing upon the ancient Christian hymn found in St. Paul's Letter to the Philippians 2:6–8. There we read of Jesus Christ, "who though he was in the form of God, did not regard equality with God as something to be exploited, but emptied himself, taking the form of a slave, being born in human likeness. And being found in human form, he humbled himself. . . ." Creation in this interpretation is to be thought of as God's self-emptying. "The best way," Hosinski thinks, "to understand creation is to think of it as God sharing the divine life with all agents in the universe, all creatures, not just with humans."[64] In a remarkably fine phrase reflecting words of Whitehead, Hosinski concludes that "we live out of the God who dwells within us. . . . The universe is not God. But just as in the incarnation God chose to share our life, perhaps the energy of the universe is God's gift of allowing us and all agents of the universe to share in God's life."[65]

63. Hosinski, *Image of the Unseen God*, 118.
64. Hosinski, *Image of the Unseen God*, 119.
65. Hosinski, *Image of the Unseen God*, 119. Although not himself a process theologian, the Franciscan Zachary Hayes, well informed by contemporary science as well as theology, writes in a way that is supportive of Hosinski: "As a God of love, God has created a world that is not ruled by force or coercion. The creative love of God can well be thought of as a power that 'let things be'; a power that calls creatures to realize the potential that lies within them. Process theology tends to think of God as the source of all possibilities; a God who does not push creatures out from a past, but who calls creatures from the future. Given the contemporary understanding of a developing cosmos, and developing species within it, and given the dynamic of development that seems to involve an interplay between chance and necessity, it might be more helpful to think of God not as the eternal Planner who has written a finished script for cosmic history which must be carried out, but rather to think of God as the Infinite Source of new possibilities. Cosmos is open to a real future, and that future finally is the fruit of cosmic and human history responding to the possibilities offered by God." See Hayes, *The Gift of Being*, 119.

Conclusion

Readers will decide for themselves just how intellectually satisfying and persuasive the insights of these representative theologians are. Different ways of understanding will appeal to people differently, depending upon their theological and philosophical presuppositions. A democratization of theology has taken place in the last half-century that has opened up all kinds of new perspectives for Christians. However, I do not wish to leave the account at the intellectual level only. At the end of the day my hope is that reading such theologians about the theology of creation, especially in an evolutionary mode, will lead to a more deeply integrated spiritual life and to a more informed understanding of the very rich Christian tradition. Theology is not only "faith seeking understanding" in the traditional definition of St. Anselm. It is also, at its best, mystagogic, that is to say, leading us more deeply into personal encounter with the living mystery of God in and through his creation, and so to the acclamation "How great Thou art!"

7

The Mystery of Evil and Suffering

Perhaps for the problem of suffering there simply is no single, comprehensive answer. Perhaps there are only various partial answers, and we are all called to construct our own, taking into account our own experience, our own suffering, as well as the precious insights of the many others who have ever wrestled with the problem. . . . Perhaps we must listen especially to those who, in spite of their great grief, have nevertheless not lost their deepest peace.

Herwig Arts[1]

The theoretical problem of theodicy, i.e. of how God can be "justified" in the face of suffering, is not new, but the Holocaust raises it to a new pitch, to breaking-point and, perhaps, beyond.

George Pattison[2]

The willingness of those who have suffered most to begin living anew bears witness to the power of creativity and hope over death and destruction.

Tina Beattie[3]

1. Arts, *God, the Christian*, 105.
2. Pattison, *End of Theology*, 8.
3. Beattie, "Where Was God?," 8.

The Mystery of Evil and Suffering

Opening Up the Mystery

THE EPIGRAPHS THAT OPEN up this chapter provide us with sound and solid orientation for exploring the challenges of evil and suffering. Herwig Arts and Tina Beattie both provide hope in the face of suffering. George Pattison sharpens the issue by introducing the Holocaust. In my judgment, there is no final intellectually satisfying answer the questions posed by the experience of evil and suffering. In any approach to the theology of creation it is impossible to evade the problem of why bad things happen to good people, to slightly modify the title of Rabbi Harold Kushner's influential book, *When Bad Things Happen to Good People* (1981). Perhaps Kushner's approach could be summarized as "people who are suffering don't need theology but sympathy."

After summarizing and responding to various kinds of theodicy, philosophical theologian James Byrne puts forward his own position:

> [Our response to suffering] depends on our reaction to our whole existence—emotional, physical, social and cognitive—and on our capacity to find some meaning in even the darkest moments. It will depend on how each of us creates meanings which sustain us through joy and sadness and it will depend on what we hope for and expect from our lives and from the universe as we experience it.[4]

Byrne talks about creating meanings that sustain us and that is surely correct up to a point, but our creating meanings is really also about finding meanings that are *already there* in our various traditions, whether cultural, philosophical, or religious. We never create meaning from nowhere. We are always somewhere, and that somewhere is a "tradition," an ever-flowing current of beliefs, values, and practices. There is so much to be said for getting to know our originating tradition better, so as to sift through with great care those beliefs, values, and practices that have, at least in part, made us who we are. When it comes to the evils and sufferings of

---

4. Byrne, *God*, 95.

life that we all must encounter and experience, this could not be more important.

Some Initial Suggestions

What response may we make to the challenges posed by evil and suffering, given that it is really impossible to reach toward an intellectually satisfying solution to the challenges? Here are some initial suggestions.

1. In his very fine book *Creation and Redemption* Gabriel Daly makes the following statement: "Any consideration of the human journey to God must at some point reckon with the problem of evil. One knows in advance that there are no answers, only an opportunity for anguished speculation."[5] "No answers," "anguished speculation"! In reality, then, this means that every person is what German philosopher Ernst Bloch called a *laboratorium beatitudinis*, a laboratory of happiness, a laboratory in which the greatest possible happiness must be sought, personally and socially, in a difficult-to-achieve integration of suffering and pain. Happiness here is not to be construed as the pursuit of an egoistic, hedonistic paradise. Rather, it should be thought of as the pursuit of a certain but necessarily limited satisfaction, a reflective-philosophical integration that enables one to go on without intellectual complacency on the one hand, but with spiritual and moral compassion in the face of suffering. This is close to what Gabriel Daly means "the terrifying asceticism of searching for meaning amid the tears of things."[6]

2. We cannot provide a detailed explanation why people suffer particular hardships. Sometimes we bring hardships upon ourselves through, for example, overindulgence in food or drink, smoking, or putting ourselves at unnecessary risk in various ways. This however, is not the case when we consider

---

5. Daly, *Creation and Redemption*, 149.
6. Daly, *Creation and Redemption*, 152.

children suffering from cancer. Perhaps in the future scientists and especially medical practitioners will provide answers or pathways through such hardship and suffering, but at this time they are not universally available.

3. Sometimes the sufferings people experience can be explained as a *means* to some greater good, as some "vast pedagogy of pain."[7] It happens that suffering can sometimes lead to a greater good in the life of a person, can, for example, lead them toward a deeper reflection on what life is all about. Suffering can help people turn to God, even re-turn to God, to bring about reconciliation in families where alienation existed, and healing in other such ways. However, that is not always the case. Sometimes people are simply utterly crushed by suffering and led to despair. Philosophical theologian Thomas Tracy seems to have it right when he says, "When harm nonetheless leads to the emergence of some good in the sufferer's life, this is a work of grace that redeems and heals, rather than an outcome built into a means/ends strategy."[8] When good things emerge from suffering, that is a work of God's grace in Tracy's terms, but it ought not to be thought of as a difficult means to a good end.

4. In Christian belief, our "good" goes beyond this life. This is so important. Christians understand life to go beyond our biological living in this world. We are made for consummation in God. "Communion with God is a good that includes and transcends the span of our biological lives; Christian faith looks in hope toward life with God beyond death."[9] This is not intended to mean that we remain in a complacent condition, either with ourselves or with others when it comes to suffering. God is the Love that will not let us go, even through what seems like the finality of death. All that is humanly possible to be done should be done to alleviate suffering. At the

---

7. Tracy, "Why Do the Innocent Suffer?," 49.
8. Tracy, "Why Do the Innocent Suffer?," 47.
9. Tracy, "Why Do the Innocent Suffer?," 48.

same time, the Christian vision recognizes that life in this world does not finally define the human person.

5. Life in final and full communion with God is not, of course, a hope only for Christians but rather in our Christian tradition it is a hope for all human persons. Writing in the wake of the 2004 Indian Ocean earthquake and tsunami, theologian Tina Beattie makes this important point: "Christians must insist that every human life is of equal value to God, whether it is an American or an Iraqi, an Oxford professor or an Indonesian fisherman, a believer or an atheist. In God, all the dead are counted and named: there are no anonymous, insignificant deaths."[10]

6. What about natural evils, earthquakes, tsunamis, and so forth? Can God not be held responsible for these? Here we are at the very edge of language, of what it is possible to say. I think we have to say God could have made a different world than this—at least the traditional grammar of God-talk and God's "power" seems to demand this—but God could not have made this particular world differently. In other words, the laws of physics and chemistry that produce glorious panoramas and awesome sunsets, for example, are the same laws that in different ways and degrees bring about natural catastrophes. "A world in which events do not fall into reliable patterns would leave us unable to form an intelligible map of its structure and therefore unable to learn or to act. If, however, the world has a stable, lawful structure, then it will be possible for us to collide with it and to be hurt in the process."[11] Collisions do occur and many people do get hurt. There is no simple, straightforward, "sound-bite" answer to natural disasters/evils. Really, when all is said and done, even as we continue to think through evil and suffering, the mystery of evil and suffering ultimately fades into the Mystery that is God, and the invitation is to trust, come what may. The line from Psalm 23

10. Beattie, "Where Was God?," 8–9.
11. Tracy, "Why Do the Innocent Suffer?," 50.

comes immediately to mind—"Even though I walk through the valley of the shadow of death, I fear no evil, for Thou art with me."

7. The reaction of people of religious faith, and indeed of all people with a moral conscience, should be always one of passionate engagement with the lives that are left after catastrophic natural evils. The human heart asks not for understanding—at least not that alone—but for ways of changing the situation in whatever ways that are open to us, even if they are very small. Former Archbishop of Canterbury Rowan Williams has wisely written: "The odd thing is that those who are most deeply involved—both as sufferers and as helpers—are so often the ones who spend least energy in raging over the lack of explanation. They are likely to shrug off, awkwardly and not very articulately, the great philosophical or religious questions we might want to press. Somehow, they are most aware of two things: a kind of strength and vision just to go on; and a sense of the imperative for practical service and love. Somehow in all of this, God simply emerges for them as a faithful presence. Arguments 'for and against' have to be put in the context of that awkward, stubborn persistence."[12]

I think it is possible for Christians to go beyond these initial suggestions, even as we accept their limited persuasiveness by turning to the Scriptures.

The Book of Job

Not too many Christians these days, I think, have read all the way through the book of Job, a post-exilic text that explores the mystery of suffering in life. "[Job] is a poetic tale that undermines and mocks all stock responses to suffering."[13] The stock response to suffering in Hebrew theology was enshrined in the law of retribution, that is, the just are rewarded, and the wicked are punished. As

---

12. Williams, "Asian Tsunami," 3.
13. Gallagher, *The Human Poetry of Faith*, 33.

the narrative opens, we are presented with a view of Job, who is not a Hebrew but from the "land of Uz," but who may be described as a just man, even a living saint. He enjoys a life of prosperity and happiness, and then a series of calamities overtakes him, and he loses everything. The entire book exposes the weaknesses of taking for granted the law of retribution. This traditional law of retribution is unable to account for all the sufferings that have befallen Job.

Job is visited by three friends, Eliphaz, Bildad, and Zophar, who are defenders of the traditional view of the law of retribution. In their view Job must have done something very bad to account for the enormity of his sufferings, and they go on to reflect on this at some length. So extreme is Job's situation that they remain in silence for a week before embarking of their religious arguments. Job listens to his friends' lengthy and tedious theological explanations for his suffering, and finally comments that silence is their only wisdom. "If you would only keep silent, that would be your wisdom!" (Job 13:5). As Job is moved to present his own reflections their content can be summarized by the old bumper sticker slogan, "Life's a bitch, and then you die."

The real problem with the friends' indictment of Job is well-expressed in the *New Jerome Biblical Commentary*: "They are not willing to leave a margin of uncertainty, to admit limits to their understanding, to write after each of their theses, 'If God so wills.' All the workings of divine providence must be clear to them, explicit, mathematical. They have fallen victims to the occupational hazard of theologians: they forget they are dealing with mystery."[14] The friends of Job and perhaps all of us at times forget we are dealing with mystery, In keeping with the international character of wisdom literature in the Old Testament the friends are non-Jews, like Job himself. Interestingly, as the three friends lecture Job directly and at length, *they never actually speak to God*. By way of contrast, Job often turns *to* God in the book. Job argues with God, and even if he cannot find God (Job 23.8–9) he never stops yearning for a confrontation, and this reaches its climax in chapter 23: "Oh, that I knew where I might find him, that I might come even to his

---

14. MacKenzie and Murphy, "Job," 467.

The Mystery of Evil and Suffering

dwelling! ... If I go forward, he is not there; or backward, I cannot perceive him; on the left he hides, and I cannot behold him; I turn to the right, but I cannot see him."

The book reaches its dramatic climax in the appearance of Yahweh, who speaks as "the voice from the storm" ("whirlwind") in Job 38:1. "Then the LORD answered Job out of the whirlwind: 'Who is this that darkens counsel by words without knowledge? Gird up your loins like a man, I will question you, and you shall declare to me.'" There are two speeches from God. The first speech (chapters 38–39) reflects on God's power over and care for creation. The second speech (40:6—41:34) focuses on God's power and care for Behemoth and Leviathan—two "mythical monsters" with superhuman powers. In these speeches God does not give answers to Job's questions about suffering. Rather, God asks questions that have the effect of overwhelming Job. Yahweh's questions to Job, overwhelming as they are, bring about Job's transformation. "The Lord's questions add little to Job's fund of knowledge, but they do leave him changed. ... It is enough for Job; vision has replaced hearsay. Job's experience of God in the theophany works the transformation that the lectures of the friends could not accomplish."[15]

Let's turn to the marvelous passage in Job 42:1–6:

> Then Job answered the LORD: "I know that you can do all things, and that no purpose of yours can be thwarted. 'Who is this that hides counsel without knowledge?' Therefore, I have uttered what I did not understand, things too wonderful for me, which I did not know. 'Hear, and I will speak; I will question you, and you declare to me.' I had heard of you by the hearing of the ear, but now my eye sees you; therefore, I despise myself, and repent in dust and ashes."

Scripture scholar Daniel Harrington poses this question about these lines: "Is it cynicism, resignation, or mystical transformation?"[16] Arguably, Job refuses to impose on God his own perspective and questions about suffering, and he has reached a point of what can

---

15. Murphy, *The Tree of Life*, 23.
16. Harrington, *Why Do We Suffer?*, 50.

best be called "mystical transformation." Philosophical theologian Santiago Sia offers us some helpful comments:

> The answer given is not to the question why the innocent Job is suffering, but to the more profound point which Job had raised: God's nature and the human being's relationship to this God. . . . Job comes to the stage where his original question of why he is suffering in spite of being innocent becomes irrelevant. He has been transformed and in the context of his changed state, that question slips into obscurity. . . . In his suffering Job experiences God differently. He wanted to know why he was suffering, but he ends up relating more to his God. He was dissatisfied with the answers provided by his friends because these were attempts to justify suffering, but what matters more is his relationship with this God.[17]

I don't think Job is being cynical, nor do I believe he is finally resigned to the fact of his suffering. Something much more is happening. Job is experiencing mystical transformation in and through his encounter with God, and this mystical transformation is taken to its most intense in the writings of St. Paul.

The Pauline Corporate Mystical Vision

What I am calling the "Pauline corporate mystical vision" is my version in terms used earlier in this chapter of a scripturally based "reflective-philosophical integration that enables one to go on without intellectual complacency on the one hand, but with spiritual and moral compassion in the face of suffering." Let's begin with two texts from 1 Corinthians:

> 1 Cor 3:17. "If anyone destroys God's temple, God will destroy him. For God's temple is holy, and that temple you are."

---

17. Sia and Sia, *From Suffering to God*, 25–26. See also the similar perspective of Gallagher, *The Human Poetry of Faith*, 54–55.

1 Cor 6:19. "Do you not know that your body is a temple of the Holy Spirit within you, which you have from God?"

In both of these texts "you" is plural in Greek, not singular. In these texts St. Paul is telling the Corinthian Christian community that they are the temple of God. To appreciate what this means we need to understand that in the ancient world the local temple dedicated to the local god was a sacred place in which the deity could be encountered. That was even more true for Jews of the temple in Jerusalem. In Paul's time the Jerusalem Temple was still standing and for Jews it was the holiest place on earth, the very dwelling place of God. Now Paul transfers something of that meaning to the Christian community itself. They are the very dwelling place of God since they have God's Spirit within them.

Christians are the temple-of-God-in-Christ. This is what I mean by "mystical transformation." This mystical faith-union of the believer with Christ is found in many Pauline passages. Sometimes, it is expressed very simply as being "in Christ." New Testament scholar Richard Hays puts it well: "Christ is personally united with his people in such a way that they become his 'body.' He is actually present in and through them.... Consequently, he manifests his identity to the world through this complex corporate reality.... The Church really is the Body of Christ, because Christ lives in us."[18] This language is truly remarkable.

This fundamental mystical union with Christ gets expressed in the Pauline literature using the Greek word *syn-*, "with, along with, together with." Consider the following examples.

Rom 6:4	*synthaptein*	to be buried with
Rom 6:6	*systarousthai*	to be crucified with
Rom 6:8	*syzein*	to live with
Rom 8:17	*sympaschein*	to suffer with
	syndoxazein	to be glorified with
	sygkleronomoi	to be joint heirs with

18. Hays, "The Story of God's Son," 195.

2 Cor 7:3	*synapothanein*	to die with
Col 2:12	*synthaptein*	to be buried with
	synegerein	to be raised with
Col 2:13	*syzoopoiein*	to be made alive with

In the light of these passages, and reflecting on all these verbs with *syn-*/"with," the mystical identity of the believer with Christ is crystal-clear, even as the language is that of paradox.

Now let's go to Galatians 2:20, linking human suffering to Christ: "I have been crucified with Christ; it is no longer I who live, but Christ lives in me; and the life which I now live in the flesh I live by faith in the Son of God, who loved me and gave himself for me." "I have been crucified with Christ"—language is almost at breaking-point here. Breaking point, yes, but this language of Paul should not be thought of as overblown or inflated, but rather as overwhelmingly paradoxical and yet fully real. The newly baptized Christian has been inserted into Christ in such a way that Christ becomes his or her most intimate identity. The New Testament scholar Morna Hooker has captured Paul's theology of grace finely when she writes, "Look at Christ and you will see what God is like; look at Christians, and what you should see is what Christ is like."[19] Taking this mystical understanding further with some comments from Rowan Williams:

> Jesus cannot be spoken of simply as an individual in the past. He is not only currently active, but the "kinship group" of which he is the common and defining "ancestor" is here and now open to his agency and growing into a different kind of existence as a result of that agency, which is "appropriated" to its human members, in the sense that what they do and say in the name or persona of Jesus counts as done or said by Jesus.[20]

This mystical vision of St. Paul, building upon the mystical transformation of Job in his encounter with God, invites us

---

19. Hooker and Young, *Holiness and Mission*, 13.
20. Williams, *Christ the Heart of Creation*, 55.

to recognize ourselves as embodied in Christ, so that as we are embodied in him we can also say that he is embodied in us. Suffering remains suffering, the evils we encounter remain the evils we encounter, but cultivating this mystical vision leads us to relate to suffering—the sufferings of the world and our own suffering—on a higher plane, indeed, the highest plane, since suffering is suffused with the divine presence of God-in-Christ. As Easter Sunday brings the darkness of Good Friday into resurrection light, so Christians believe that they too will have their Easter Sunday as God draws them through the darkness of their individual Good Fridays. What I am calling the mystical vision of St. Paul holds this hope firmly before us.

St. Augustine and Benedict of Canfield

The mystical identification with Christ remains a constant throughout the Christian tradition. It is found everywhere, in the Greek East and the Latin West, in every generation. To illustrate, let us call upon two witnesses, St. Augustine of Hippo and Benedict of Canfield. For Augustine, the Psalms form the language of confession—"confession" for him is the very action that unites us to Christ.[21] Thus, we read of Augustine confessing Christ in the Psalms, for example, as follows:

> God could have granted no greater gift to human beings than to cause his Word, through whom he created all things, to be their head, and to fit them to him as his members. He was thus to be Son of God and Son of Man, one God with the Father, one human being with us. The consequence is that when we speak to God in prayer we do not separate the Son from God, and when the body of the Son prays it does not separate its head from itself. The one sole savior of his body is our Lord Jesus Christ, the Son of God, who prays for us, prays in us, and is prayed

---

21. See Grove, *Augustine on Memory*, 59–62.

to by us. He prays for us as our priest, he prays in us as our head, and he is prayed to by us as our God.[22]

Taking yet another Augustinian passage we read:

> Accordingly, when we hear his voice, we must hearken to it as coming from both head and body; for whatever he suffered, we too suffered in him; and it follows that now that he has ascended into heaven and is seated at the Father's right hand, he still undergoes in the person of the church whatever it may suffer amid the troubles of the world, whether temptations, or hardship or oppression.[23]

The magnificent Pauline vision of our identity in Christ runs throughout Augustine's works. There is no Christ without the church, and there is no church without Christ, and we are that embodiment in Christ, to be distinguished but never separated.

My final illustration of this mystical vision comes from the little known late sixteenth- and early seventeenth-century mystic Benedict of Canfield, OFM Cap. He writes in his 1609 *Rule of Perfection*:

> Therefore our own pains—insofar as they are not ours but those of Christ—must be deeply respected. How wonderful! And more: our pains are as much to be revered as those of Jesus Christ in His own passion. For if people correctly adore Him with so much devotion in images on the Good Friday cross, why may we not then revere Him on the living cross that we ourselves are?[24]

This mystical vision has never been forgotten. How could it be, given the Scriptures and the sacraments of the church that underscore it? In my opinion, however, two historical events

---

22. St. Augustine, "Exposition of Psalm 85, 1," III/18.
23. St. Augustine, "Exposition of Psalm 85, 1," 62, 2.
24. I owe this reference to Benedict of Canfield to Arts, *God, the Christian, and Human Suffering*, 74. Arts goes on to comment as follows: "The mystics, then, never hesitate to consider their own sufferings as a precious treasure, for that suffering is the shrine in which they bear God in themselves: 'The perfect see God in all things, but all the more in the sufferings . . . in which He is present in such an exceptional way.'"

"dislocated" the vision. First were the sixteenth-century Reformations. The Christian world became involved in "intra-mural" disputes about ecclesiology, the sacramental life, and so forth. The vision remained, but intellectual energies tended to be engaged in polemics, Catholics and Reformation Christians "doing theology against one another." Second was the eighteenth-century philosophical movement known as the Enlightenment. Think, for example, of Immanuel Kant's dictum *Sapere aude*, "Think for yourself!" One consequence was the massive movement away from tradition, when "thinking *for* yourself" became identified with "thinking *by* yourself." Rationalism and individualism ruled. God-in-Christ-through the Spirit—always mystically conjoined with creation/humankind and most especially in the Christ-church—was relegated to heaven, became a "deity," that is to say "something" even a "divine Something," rather than the Triune Mystery and creative-redeeming Source of all that is. Questions changed. Does this Supreme Something really exist? Can his existence be "proved" rationally? How do you reconcile evil and suffering with a God who is all-good and all-powerful? Philosophical theodicies, in contrast to the mystical vision, experienced a renaissance.

Practice, Practice, Practice!

This paradoxical mystical vision of union with Christ-in-God is difficult enough to put into a form of words, even if those words come from Holy Scripture. If they are to be really meaningful to someone who is going through serious suffering, the vision has to be worked at. In some fine words of theologian Christopher Baglow, this mystical vision of union with Christ-in-God "is a hope that calls on the love of God within, transforming me into one who, like Christ, finds salvation within suffering, who learns compassion and the courage not only to suffer but to suffer valiantly with others."[25]

---

25. Baglow, *Creation*, 28.

The vision has to be cultivated on a regular basis, and I would argue on a daily basis. This means cultivating Christian faith primarily as a set of practices, a set of practices that cumulatively will assist in the mystical transformation of our lives.[26] What practices? A hierarchy of practices beginning with genuine friendship with others. Learning to encounter others as, we may say, "God-present." Add to this very ordinary practice of cultivating friendship the practice of habitual prayer, the raising up of the mind and heart to God, the contemplation of regular wonder, of being "wowed" by the Mystery that is God. Practicing gratitude, the gratitude that gives thanks for the gift of life, for the many daily acts of kindness and of love. Practicing generosity toward other so less fortunate. Practicing forgiveness—"Forgive us our trespasses as we forgive those who trespass against us." Practicing especially Eucharist through which our bond with Christ-in-God and simultaneously our bond with all humankind is deepened and strengthened.

---

26. Consider especially the emphasis on practice in the recent work of Hector, *Christianity as a Way of Life*.

8

Conclusion

> *Everything lives, moves, and has its being in God. Everything is grace, everything gift. The world is not random chaos but good. God is not nowhere but everywhere. This may be a hard teaching in times of pain, but the alternative is far worse.*
>
> Janet M. Soskice[1]

As I was putting the finishing touches to this book, I came across the following words from systematic theologian Christopher Baglow:

> The universe we live in is subject to a narrative, although we do not know all the details of that narrative. Just like salvation history, the universe has a purpose toward which it has been moving, in fits and starts, since whenever it began. And the story of our salvation is to that longer narrative the decisive turning point, the chapter which reveals what the whole story is about.[2]

What he has to say is very good. The universe of every person we may say is subject to a narrative. Everyone lives from a story of

---

1. Soskice, "Why Creatio ex Nihilo for Theology Today?," 52.
2. Baglow, *Creation*, 13.

how things are. No one knows all the details of their narrative. With basic trust in our received narratives, but a trust refined through the experiences of the life cycle, we are all invited to live out of this fundamental trust.

Having spent some time thinking about the Christian doctrine of creation, and of our trust in it, I think we may summarize the doctrine fundamentally as follows: God creates the universe from nothing, with time, freely, and as Triune. The epigraph from Janet Soskice is saying the same thing, albeit in a more pleasing fashion. In her final sentence we find a way forward in respect of the challenges of evil, pain, and suffering. This is where trust in our Christian narrative is especially helpful—"This may be a hard teaching in times of pain, but the alternative us far worse."

St. Paul writes, "We know that all things work together for good for those who love God, who are called according to his purpose" (Rom 8:28). We do not know exactly how this happens in every single instance, but it is a fundamental conviction of Christians. It grounds and forms the basis of our understanding of all reality, of our trust-narrative. This fundamental conviction flows from the axiom that "God is love" (1 John 4:16). The least inadequate name for God is "Love." Everything comes from this God-who-is-Love and at the parousia, the End, will return to him, perfected and made whole. We have no clear idea of exactly what this means. We have no clear idea of how God-who-is-Love will draw all creation to its final perfection. That fundamental conviction, however, despite the necessary ambiguity surrounding it, remains firm and strong. It remains firm and strong not just in the big picture concerning all creation, but also in the small picture of our human lives, and most especially through "practice." The conviction will evaporate without the constancy of practice. We live in and from hope, and that hope perdures through everything—the joys, works, and sufferings of every day. That is why, for St. Paul, love is the greatest of the gifts (1 Cor 12–13). This is love (small case) as self-donation, and Love (capital letter) as self-donation, "the deepest etymology of love," and it is the motive for everything

Conclusion

that exists on the part of God who donates-creates, and on the part of the human person who donates-responds.³

Thus, God is not present to reality, to creation, nor to us, as an external force, even a beneficent force, among other forces. God is not another existing reality over against all the other realities around us. It has been well expressed by John H. Wright: God is present and active "in the within of all things in the universe. He is present in their within, acting to realize his purposes everywhere." Wright is not saying that God *is* the within of all things—that would be a reductionist pantheism. Rather he is saying that God is *in the within* of all things.

> All things are "from him," for he is the source of the reality of all things. All things are "through him" and "in him," for he is the ultimate support of their being and activity. All things are "to him," for he is the attractive impulse drawing them into the future, building them up through the evolutionary process into more and more complex material arrangements and, corresponding to them, more and more intense centers of inwardness or consciousness.⁴

These few sentences are powerful and invite slow, personal appropriation. God out of sheer generosity and goodness (= Love as self-donation) draws us and all creation from nothing to existence. Indeed, "God" is the answer to the question, "Why is there anything at all rather than nothing?" Or, more existentially and personally, "Why am I?"

Recapitulating ideas found throughout this book, the Christian answer is "God," that is, Love (1 John 4:16). Using the words of St. Thomas Aquinas, and before him of the anonymous Syrian theologian whom we know as Pseudo-Dionysius, "Goodness is diffusive of itself."⁵ Maybe at first the notion that "Goodness is diffusive of itself" sounds very abstract, but it isn't really. It is a

---

3. Whelan, *Benjamin*, 11, 30.

4. Wright, *Theology of Christian Prayer*, 45–49.

5. St. Thomas Aquinas, *Summa Theologiae*, Ia.27,4; Pseudo-Dionysius, *On the Divine Names*, IV.20.

self-authenticating principle. We all probably know good people, loving people in whose company we like to linger. Their generosity, both in word and action, radiates a sense of well-being. We not only react positively to such people, we also intuit and trust that such generosity/goodness is somehow foundational to reality, the very heart of reality we might say. That's what I mean by saying that it is self-authenticating. The self-authentication that flows from encounters with such goodness can, I believe, be further built-up through reflection. That can be helpful, but it seems to me not necessary. Experiencing "goodness-diffusive-of-itself" is spontaneously recognized as somehow "just right," and it evokes similar "goodness-diffusive-of-itself" in us. This points to God, the God who creates us for communion. This is the God who evokes adoration and praise, the awareness of whom invites contrition and sorrow on our part for those things we regret, but much more whose unbounded generosity in creating elicits thanksgiving and praise as we pray, "How great Thou art!"

Bibliography

Anderson, Gary A. "Creatio ex Nihilo and the Bible." In *Creation ex Nihilo: Origins, Development, Contemporary Challenges*, edited by Gary Anderson and Markus Bockmuehl, 15–36. Notre Dame, IN: University of Notre Dame Press, 2018.

Anderson, Gary A., and Markus Bockmuehl, eds. *Creation ex Nihilo: Origins, Development, Contemporary Challenges*. Notre Dame, IN: University of Notre Dame Press, 2018.

Armstrong, Regis J., et al., eds. *Francis and Clare: The Complete Works*. Mahwah, NJ: Paulist, 1986.

Arts, Herwig. *God, the Christian, and Human Suffering*. Collegeville, MN: Liturgical, 1993.

Augustine. "Exposition of Psalm 85, 1." In *The Works of St. Augustine: A Translation for the 21st Century, Expositions of the Psalms*, III/18. Hyde Park, NY: New City, 2002.

Baglow, Christopher T. *Creation, A Catholic's Guide to God and the Universe*. Notre Dame, IN: Ave Maria, 2021.

Bauckham, Richard. *The Bible and Ecology: Rediscovering the Community of Creation*. London: Darton, Longman and Todd, 2010.

Beattie, Tina. "Where Was God?" *The Tablet*, January 8, 2005, 8.

Bergquist, Anders. "Gnosticism." In *Heresies and How to Avoid Them*, edited by Ben Quash et al., 102–12. Peabody, MA: Hendrickson, 2007.

Blankenhorn, Bernhard-Thomas. "The Good as Self-Diffusive in Thomas Aquinas." *Angelicum* 79 (2002) 803–37.

Blowers, Paul M. "Creation." In *The Oxford Handbook of Early Christian Biblical Interpretation*, edited by Paul M. Blowers and Peter W. Martens, 15–26. Oxford: Oxford University Press, 2019.

———. *Drama of the Divine Economy: Creator and Creation in Early Christian Theology and Piety*. Oxford: Oxford University Press, 2012.

Blowers, Paul M., and Robert Wilken. *On the Cosmic Mystery of Jesus Christ: Selected Writings from St. Maximus the Confessor*. Crestwood, NY. St. Vladimir's Seminary Press, 2003.

BIBLIOGRAPHY

Brueggemann, Walter. *Israel's Praise: Doxology against Idolatry and Ideology*. Philadelphia: Fortress, 1988.

Butterfield, Herbert. *The Origins of Modern Science*. Rev. ed. New York: Free Press, 1957.

Butterworth, Robert. *The Theology of Creation*. Cork, Ireland: Mercier, 1969.

Byrne, James. *God*. New York: Continuum, 2001.

Carroll, Denis. "Creation." In *The New Dictionary of Theology*, edited by Joseph A. Komonchak et al., 246–58. Collegeville, MN: Liturgical, 1987.

———. "An Essay in the Theology of Creation: Gabriel Daly and the Challenge of Modernity." In *The Critical Spirit: Theology at the Crossroads of Faith and Culture*, edited by Andrew Pierce and Geraldine Smyth, 15–26. Dublin: Columba, 2003.

———. *Towards a Story of the Earth: Essays on the Theology of Creation*. Dublin: Dominican, 1987.

Catechism of the Catholic Church. Washington, DC: USCCB, 1995.

Collins, John J. *Does the Bible Justify Violence?* Minneapolis: Fortress, 2004.

———. *Introduction to the Hebrew Bible*. 2nd ed. Minneapolis: Fortress, 2014.

Costley, Angela. *Creation and Christ: An Exploration of the Topic of Creation in the Epistle to the Hebrews*. Tübingen: Mohr Siebeck, 2021.

Cummings, Owen F. *Eucharistic Doctors*. Mahwah, NJ: Paulist, 2005.

———. *John Macquarrie: A Master of Theology*. Mahwah, NJ: Paulist, 2002.

———. *The Theology of John Macquarrie (1919–2007): A Comprehensive and Contextual Exploration*. Lewiston, NY: Mellen, 2010.

Daly, Gabriel. *Creation and Redemption*. Dublin: Gill and Macmillan, 1988.

de Chardin, Pierre Teilhard. *The Divine Milieu*. London: Collins, 1964.

———. *The Phenomenon of Man*. New York: Harper & Row, 1959.

Delio, Ilia. *The Emergent Christ*. Maryknoll, NY: Orbis, 2011.

de Lubac, Henri. *Teilhard de Chardin: The Man and His Meaning*. New York: New American Library, 1965.

Edwards, Denis. *Deep Incarnation*. Maryknoll, NY: Orbis, 2019.

Ellis, Peter. *The Yahwist: The Bible's First Theologian*. Notre Dame, IN: Fides 1968.

Ehr, D. J. "Creation, Theology of." In *New Catholic Encyclopedia*, 4:420–22. New York: McGraw Hill, 1967.

Eriugena, John Scotus. *Periphyseon*. Translated by John J. O'Meara. Montreal: Editions Bellarmin, 1987.

Faricy, Robert L. *Teilhard de Chardin's Theology of the Christian in the World*. New York: Sheed and Ward, 1967.

Fergusson, David. *Creation*. Grand Rapids: Eerdmans, 2014.

Ford, David F. *The Gospel of John: A Theological Commentary*. Grand Rapids: Baker, 2021.

Gallagher, Michael Paul. *The Human Poetry of Faith*. Mahwah, NJ: Paulist, 2003.

Galloway, Allan D. *Faith in a Changing Culture*. London: Allen and Unwin, 1968.

———. *Wolfhart Pannenberg*. London: Allen and Unwin, 1973.

BIBLIOGRAPHY

Gavin, John F. *A Celtic Christology: The Incarnation According to John Scotus Eriugena.* Eugene, OR: Cascade, 2014.

Gilson, Étienne. *History of Christian Philosophy in the Middle Ages.* New York: Random, 1955.

Grove, Kevin G. *Augustine on Memory.* Oxford: Oxford University Press, 2021.

Gunton, Colin E. "The Doctrine of Creation." In *The Cambridge Companion to Christian Doctrine*, edited by Colin E. Gunton, 141–57. Cambridge: Cambridge University Press, 1997.

Haight, Roger. *Faith and Evolution.* Maryknoll, NY: Orbis, 2019.

———. *Jesus, Symbol of God.* Maryknoll, NY: Orbis, 2000.

Hardy, Daniel Wayne, and David F. Ford. *Jubilate, Theology in Praise.* London: Darton, Longman and Todd, 1984.

Harrington, Daniel. *Why Do We Suffer? A Scriptural Approach to the Human Condition.* Lanham, MD: Rowman and Littlefield, 2000.

Hawkins, D. J. B. *A Sketch of Medieval Philosophy.* New York: Sheed and Ward, 1947.

Hayes, Zachary. *The Gift of Being: A Theology of Creation.* Collegeville, MN: Liturgical, 2001.

Hays, Richard B. "The Story of God's Son: The Identity of Jesus in the Letters of Paul." In *Seeking the Identity of Jesus*, edited by Beverly Roberts Gaventa and Richard B. Hays, 180–99. Grand Rapids: Eerdmans, 2008.

Hector, Kevin. *Christianity as a Way of Life: A Systematic Theology.* New Haven, CT: Yale University Press, 2023.

Hibbs, Thomas S. *A Theology of Creation.* Notre Dame, IN: University of Notre Dame Press, 2023.

Hooker, Morna, and Frances Young. *Holiness and Mission.* London: SCM, 2010.

Hosinski, Thomas E. *The Image of the Unseen God.* Maryknoll, NY: Orbis, 2017.

Irwin, Kevin. *A Commentary on Laudato Si: Examining the Background, Contributions, Implementation, and the Future of Pope Francis's Encyclical.* Mahwah, NJ: Paulist, 2016.

———. *Ecology, Liturgy and the Sacraments.* Mahwah, NJ: Paulist, 2022.

Johnson, Elizabeth A. *Ask the Beasts: Darwin and the God of Love.* New York: Bloomsbury 2015.

———. *Creation and the Cross.* Maryknoll, NY: Orbis, 2018.

Julian of Norwich. *Julian of Norwich, Showings.* Edited by Edmund Colledge. New York-Mahwah, NJ: Paulist, 1977.

Kaufman, Gordon D. *In Face of Mystery: A Constructive Theology.* Cambridge: Harvard University Press, 1993.

———. *In the Beginning—Creativity.* Minneapolis: Fortress, 2004.

Kelly, John N. D. *Early Christian Doctrines.* Rev. ed. Peabody, MA: Hendrickson, 2003.

Laishley, Joseph. "Image of Redemptive Love." *The Way* 23 (1983) 87–101.

Lane, Dermot A. *Nature Praising God: Towards a Theology of the Natural World.* Dublin: Messenger, 2022.

———. *Theology and Ecology in Dialogue: The Wisdom of Laudato Si*. Dublin: Messenger, 2020.
Lash, Nicholas. "Are we Born and Do We Die?" *New Blackfriars* 90 (2009) 403–12.
Le Goff, Jacques. *Saint Francis of Assisi*. London: Routledge, 2004.
Lonergan, Bernard J. F. *Insight*. London: Longmans Green, 1958.
———. *Method in Theology*. New York: Herder, 1972.
Lukas, Mary, and Ellen Lukas. *Teilhard: A Biography*. London: Collins, 1977.
MacKenzie, R. A. F., and R. E. Murphy. "Job." In *The New Jerome Biblical Commentary*, edited by R. E. Brown et al., 398–481. Englewood Cliffs, NJ: Prentice-Hall, 1990.
Mackey, James P. *The Scientist and the Theologian: On the Origin and Ends of Creation*. Dublin: Columba, 2007.
Macquarrie, John. *God and Secularity*. Philadelphia: Westminster, 1967.
———. *The Humility of God*. London: SCM, 1978.
———. *In Search of Deity*. New York: Crossroad, 1984.
———. *Principles of Christian Theology*. London: SCM, 1977.
———. *Two Worlds Are Ours: An Introduction to Christian Mysticism*. Minneapolis: Fortress, 2005.
Madigan, Kevin. *Medieval Christianity: A New History*. New Haven, CT: Yale University Press, 2015.
Masterson, Patrick. *In Reasonable Hope: Philosophic Reflections on Ultimate Meaning*. Washington, DC: Catholic University of America Press, 2021.
Maximus the Confessor. *On the Cosmic Mystery of Jesus Christ*. Translated with an introduction by Paul M. Blowers and Robert Louis Wilken. Crestwood, NY: St. Vladimir's Seminary Press, 2003.
McCabe, Herbert. *God Matters*. London: Chapman, 1987.
McCool, Gerald A., ed. *The Universe as Journey: Conversations with W. Norris Clarke, S.J*. New York: Fordham University Press, 1988.
McGinn, Bernard. *The Growth of Mysticism*. New York: Crossroad, 1996.
McGinn, Bernard, and Willemien Otten. *Eriugena, East and West*. Notre Dame, IN: University of Notre Dame Press, 1994.
McKenzie, John L. *Dictionary of the Bible*. Milwaukee: Bruce, 1965.
Moran, Dermot. *The Philosophy of John Scotus Eriugena*. Cambridge: Cambridge University Press, 1989.
Moriarty, John. *Serious Sounds*. Dublin: Lilliput, 2007.
Murphy, Roland E. *The Gift of the Psalms*. Peabody, MA: Hendrickson, 2000.
———. *The Tree of Life: An Exploration of Wisdom Literature*. 2nd ed. Grand Rapids: Eerdmans, 1996.
Nichols, Aidan. *Singing-Masters: Church Fathers from Greek East and Latin West*. San Francisco: Ignatius, 2022.
Oliver, Simon. *Creation, A Guide for the Perplexed*. London: Bloomsbury, 2017.
O'Meara, John. J. *Eriugena*. Oxford: Clarendon, 1988.
Osborne, Kenan B. *The Franciscan Intellectual Tradition*. St. Bonaventure, NY: St. Bonaventure University, 2003.

BIBLIOGRAPHY

Pattison, George. *The End of Theology and the Task of Thinking about God.* London: SCM, 1998.
Pius XII, Pope. *Humani Generis.* Vatican City, 1950.
Polkinghorne, John. "Kenotic Creation and Divine Action." In *The Work of Love: Creation as Kenosis*, edited by John Polkinghorne, 90–106. Grand Rapids: Eerdmans, 2001.
———. *Science and the Trinity.* New Haven, CT: Yale University Press, 2004.
Ratzinger, Joseph. *"In the Beginning . . .": A Catholic Understanding of the Story of Creation and the Fall.* Grand Rapids: Eerdmans, 1995.
Rolston, Holmes, III. "Kenosis and Nature." In *The Work of Love: Creation as Kenosis*, edited by John Polkinghorne, 43–65. Grand Rapids: Eerdmans, 2001.
Scheffczyk, Leo. *Creation and Providence.* New York: Herder, 1970.
Sia, Marian F., and Santiago Sia. *From Suffering to God.* New York: St. Martin's, 1994.
Soskice, Janet M. *Naming God: Addressing the Divine in Philosophy, Theology and Scripture.* Cambridge: Cambridge University Press, 2023.
———. "Why *Creatio ex Nihilo* for Theology Today?" In *Creation ex Nihilo: Origins, Development, Contemporary Challenges*, edited by Gary A. Anderson et al., 37–54. Notre Dame, IN: University of Notre Dame Press, 2018.
Stuhlmueller, Carroll. *The Spirituality of the Psalms.* Collegeville, MN: Liturgical, 2002.
Tanner, Norman P., ed. *Decrees of the Ecumenical Councils.* Vol. 2. Washington, DC: Georgetown University Press, 1990.
Tilby, Angela. "Marcionism." In *Heresies and How to Avoid Them*, edited by Ben Quash et al., 73–80. Peabody, MA: Hendrickson, 2007.
Tracy, Thomas F. "Why Do the Innocent Suffer?" In *Why Are We Here?*, edited by Ronald F. Thiemann et al., 40–55. Harrisburg, PA: Trinity, 1998.
Ward, H. Clifton. "Marcion and His Critics." In *Early Christian Biblical Interpretation*, edited by Paul M. Blowers et al., 366–82. Oxford: Oxford University Press, 2019.
Ward, Keith. *Pascal's Fire: Scientific Faith and Religious Understanding.* Oxford: Oneworld 2006.
Wawrykow, Joseph. "Aquinas and Bonaventure on Creation." In *Creation ex Nihilo: Origins, Development, Contemporary Challenges*, edited by Gary A. Anderson et al., 173–94. Notre Dame, IN: University of Notre Dame Press, 2018.
Webster, John. "Creation, Doctrine of." In *The Blackwell Encyclopedia of Christian Thought*, edited by Alister McGrath, 95–97. Oxford: Blackwell, 1993.
Whelan, Joseph P. *Benjamin: Essays in Prayer.* New York: Newman 1972.
Williams, Anna M. "The Traditionalist *malgré lui*: de Chardin and Ressourcement." In *Ressourcement: A Movement for Renewal in Twentieth-*

Century Catholic Theology, edited by Gabriel Flynn et al., 111–24. Oxford: Oxford University Press, 2012.

Williams, Rowan D. "Article on the Asian Tsunami for the Sunday Telegraph." http://www.archbishopofcanterbury.org/sermons_speeches, 3.

———. *On Christian Theology*. Oxford: Blackwell, 2000.

———. *Christ the Heart of Creation*. London: Bloomsbury, 2018.

Wood, Jordan D. *The Whole Mystery of Christ: Creation as Incarnation in Maximus Confessor*. Notre Dame, IN: University of Notre Dame Press, 2022.

Wright, John H. *A Theology of Christian Prayer*. New York: Pueblo, 1979.

Young, Frances M. *God's Presence: A Contemporary Recapitulation of Early Christianity*. Cambridge: Cambridge University Press, 2013.

www.ingramcontent.com/pod-product-compliance
Lightning Source LLC
Chambersburg PA
CBHW031345160426
43196CB00007B/740